DISCOURSE

ON THE

Life and Character

OF THE

HON. LITTLETON WALLER TAZEWELL,

DELIVERED IN THE

FREEMASON STREET BAPTIST CHURCH,

BEFORE THE

BAR OF NORFOLK, VIRGINIA, AND THE CITIZENS GENERALLY,

ON THE 29TH DAY OF JUNE, 1860,

BY

HUGH BLAIR GRIGSBY, LL.D.,

MEMBER OF THE AMERICAN PHILOSOPHICAL SOCIETY, OF THE HISTORICAL SOCIETIES OF VIRGINIA, PENNSYLVANIA, ETC., ETC.

NORFOLK:

PUBLISHED BY J. D. GHISELIN, JUN.,

No. 6 WEST MAIN STREET.

1860.

DISCOURSE.

Gentlemen of the Bar:

When the sad event occurred which has drawn us together this morning, you met in your accustomed hall, and expressed the feelings which such an event might well inspire. You then adjourned to assist in performing the last solemn rites over the bier of your departed friend. Clad in mourning, you attended his remains from his residence to the steamer, and, embarking with them, transported them over the waters of that noble bay which our venerable friend had crossed so often, and of which he was so justly proud as the Mediterranean of the Commonwealth; and, in the deepening shadows of the night which had overtaken you, and which were rendered yet deeper by the glare of the solitary candles flickering in the wind, more touching by the ceremonies of religion, by the grief of his slaves, and by the smothered wailing of his children and grandchildren, and more imposing by the sorrowing faces and bent forms of some of our aged and most eminent citizens, you deposited the honored dust in its simple grave; there to repose—with two seas sounding their ceaseless requiem above it—till the trump of the Archangel shall smite the ear of the dead, and the tomb shall unveil its bosom, and the old and the young, the rich and the poor, the statesman who ruled the destinies of empires, and the peasant whose thoughts never strayed beyond his daily walk, shall rise together on the Morn of the Resurrection.

But you rightly deemed that your duty to the memory of your

illustrious brother did not cease at his grave. You knew that, whatever may be the estimate of the value of the life and services of LITTLETON WALLER TAZEWELL, it was never denied by his contemporaries that he was endowed with an extraordinary intellect, and that in popular assemblies, at the Bar, in the House of Delegates, and in the Senate of the United States, if he did not—as it was long the common faith in Virginia to believe that he did—bear away the palm from every competitor, he had few equals, and hardly in any department in which he chose to appear, a superior. And you thought that such a life, so intimately connected with your profession, deserved a special commemoration; that its leading facts should be recalled to the public mind; and that you might thus not only refresh your own recollections by the lessons presented by so remarkable a career, but hand down, if possible, whatever of instruction and encouragement and delight those lessons may contain, for the eye of those who are to succeed you. Your only error—and I speak from the heart—is in the hands to which you have confided the task.

The time for performing this duty has arrived; and I rejoice to see associated with you the Mayor and the Recorder of the City, the gentlemen of the Common and Select Councils, the officers of the army and navy, the President, Professors, and Students of William and Mary College, his venerable *alma mater*, and various public bodies distinguished by their useful and benevolent purposes. It is meet that it should be so. At the call of your fathers, gentlemen, he was ever prompt to render any service in his power; and on two occasions especially, when important interests affecting Norfolk were in jeopardy, at great pecuniary sacrifices on his part, he was sent abroad to protect them. On another occasion, when a foreign fleet was in our waters, he undertook the errand of your fathers, and performed it with unequalled success. It was in the service of your fathers that he won his great reputation as a lawyer; and to them and to you, disregarding the obvious dictates of personal interest and ambition, he clung for almost two-thirds of a century, as to his friends and neighbors, and to your city as the abode of his brilliant manhood, and the home of his declining years; and he has left his children and grandchildren, those dear objects of his love on whom his eyes rested in the dying hour, to live and to die among you. Indeed, so intimately connected was his name with the name of your city for sixty years, the first words that rose on the lips of travelled men in our own country and in England, were inquiries respecting Mr. Tazewell. The generation of men who smiled at his wit, whose tears flowed at his bidding, who relished his wonderful colloquial powers, who regarded with a sense of personal triumph his marvellous displays at the Bar and in the public councils, and who looked up to him in the hour of danger as their bulwark and defence, have, with here and there a solitary exception, long preceded him to the tomb. Those men were your fathers. He pérformed the last sad rites at their graves, as, one by one, year after year, they passed away ; and you, their sons and successors, and, I rejoice to add, their daughters and granddaughters, have now met to pay a tribute to his memory. To honor the illustrious dead is a noble and a double office. It speaks with one accord and in a language not to be mistaken, the worth of those who have gone before us, and the worth of those who yet survive.

In contemplating a human life which is older than the Commonwealth in which we live—a life stretching almost from century to century, and that century embracing the American Revolution, and sweeping yet onward with its unexpired term beyond the present moment—even if the humblest figure filled the canvas, the review of its history would far exceed the time allotted for my present office ; but if that figure be prominent, if he made his mark upon some of the great events of his age, or influenced the opinions of masses of men, or moved before them in any remarkable attitude of genius, of massive intellect, or of public service, the task is proportionably enlarged. And the only method that is left us is to point out the striking traits of the general portraiture, and to let the minor incidents take care of themselves. It is in such a spirit I shall treat the theme you have assigned me.

It appears to me that the life of Mr. Tazewell may be divided into three striking periods : The first, extending from his birth to his settlement in Norfolk in 1802 ; the second, from the settlement in Norfolk to the close of his term as Governor of the Commonwealth ; and the third, thence to his death.

It is common to associate the birth of an eminent man with the memorable events that were contemporaneous with it, and to dwell upon the influence which those events may be supposed to have exerted upon his life and character. In this respect the life of Mr. Tazewell was remarkable. Four months before the seventeenth day of December, 1774, when he was born, his father had been present at the August Convention of 1774, the first of our early conventions, which deputed Peyton Randolph, George Washington, Patrick Henry, Edward Pendleton, Benjamin Harrison, and Richard Henry Lee to the first Congress which met in Carpenter's Hall, Philadelphia, and but two months had elapsed since the adjournment of the Congress; and while the infant was in the nurse's arms, his father was drawing, probably in the same room with him, a reply to the conciliatory propositions of Lord North, to be offered in the House of Burgesses. His youthful ears were stunned by the firing of the guns of the Virginia regiments drawn up in Waller's Grove, when the news of the passage by Congress of the Declaration of Independence of the Fourth of July, 1776, reached Williamsburgh; and, as he was beginning to walk, he was startled by the roar of cannon when the victory of Saratoga was celebrated with every demonstration of joy throughout the land. As a boy of seven he heard the booming of the distant artillery at Yorktown; and he might have seen the faces of the old and the young brightening with hope, when the Articles of Confederation, which preceded the present Federal Constitution, having been ratified at last by all the States, became the first written charter of the American Union. In his ninth year the treaty of peace with Great Britain, which acknowledged the independence of the United States, was ratified by Congress; and in his fourteenth, when he remembered with distinctness current events of a political nature, the Commonwealth of Virginia adopted the present Federal Constitution.

The first of the Tazewells, who emigrated to the colony of Virginia, was William, a lawyer by profession, who came over in 1715, and settled in Accomack. He was the son of James Tazewell, of Somersetshire, England, and was born at Lymington in that county, and baptized, as appears from an extract from the register of that parish in my possession, on the 17th day of July, 1690; and was twenty-five years old on his arrival in the colony.

Wills of wealthy persons, which are still preserved in his handwriting, attest his early employment; and his name soon appears in the records of Accomack, on one or the other side of every case in court. Within the precincts of Lymington church, whose antique tower and rude structure, typifying in the graphic picture struck off by the Camden society what the old church at Jamestown probably was, may be seen the tomb of a Tazewell, who died in 1706, on which is engraved the coat of arms of the family,—a lion rampant, bearing a helmet with a vizor closed on his back; an escutcheon, which is evidently of Norman origin, and won by some daring feat of arms, and which could only have been held by one of the conquering race. A wing of the present manor-house of Lymington, built by James Tazewell, the father of William, who died in 1683, is still standing.

The orthography of Tazewell, like that of the earlier Norman names which were forced to float for centuries on the breath of the unpolished Anglo-Saxon, has been spelt at various times in various ways by members of the same family, and in various ways in the same writing; as the name of Shakspeare, though a plain Anglo-Saxon name, was spelt in four different ways in his will. Thus, in the parish register of Buckland Newton, in the county of Dorset, the name is spelt in four different ways; and one of the spellings, which is still popular in England, is Tanswell, and opens up to us the true original of the name in Tankersville, the name of one of the knights who came over with William the Norman, and whose name is inscribed on the roll of Battle Abbey. The process was evidently Tankersville, which, contracted, and marked by the apostrophe, became Tan'sville; and, as the Norman blood became, in the course of centuries, more intimately commingled with the ruder but steadier Anglo-Saxon stream, the Norman *ville* gave way to the Saxon *well*, and Tan'sville took the form of Tanswell; and Tanswell and Tazewell, variously spelt, have been used indifferently by father and son of the same family for more than three hundred years, and are so used at the present day.* The late Mr. Tazewell thought that his name was originally spelt Tazouille, and

* The various spellings are Tan'swell, Ta'rswell, Tassell, Taswell, Tazewell. Tarswell is another abbreviation of Tankersville.

that the ancestor emigrated from France to England before the revocation of the edict of Nantes, and I leaned to this opinion on another occasion ; but, apart from the absence of all evidence to sustain this opinion, it is now certain, from the autobiography of the Rev. William Tazewell, translated from the original Latin by his grandson, the Rev. Henry Tazewell, Vicar of Marden, Herefordshire, and published by the Camden Society in 1852, that the family of Tazewell flourished in England at least a century before religious disputes drew to a head in the reign of Louis the Fourteenth. I have been particular in stating these facts, as they illustrate the history of races, especially of those races which composed the people of Virginia at the date of the Revolution ; and it is something to know, that a descendant of one of those men, who, under William the Conqueror, wrested the empire of England from the successor of Alfred, and trod down beneath their iron hoofs the Anglo-Saxon people, aided in rescuing the colony of Virginia from the tyranny of George the Third, the inheritor of the blood as well as of the crown of the Norman robber.

Soon after the arrival of William Tazewell in Virginia, he married Sophia, daughter of Henry Harmanson and Gertrude Littleton, who was a daughter of Col. Southey Littleton, and the son of that marriage was called Littleton, after the surname of his grandfather. This Littleton was brought up in the secretary's office, under Secretary Nelson, and married Mary Gray, daughter of Col. Joseph Gray, of Southampton. With a view of being near the relations of his wife, he sold his estate in Accomack, which has long been the property of his grandson, Littleton Waller, and purchased land in Brunswick, of which county he became clerk of the court, dying at the early age of thirty-three. The son of this marriage was Henry, the father of our departed townsman, who also studied law, became a judge of the general court, a judge of the court of appeals, a senator of the United States, and twice president of the senate.

The mother of Mr. Tazewell was Dorothea Elizabeth Waller, a daughter of Judge Benjamin Waller, of Williamsburg. We are told by Dr. Johnson, in the Lives of the Poets, that Benjamin, the eldest son of the poet Waller, was disinherited by his father as wanting common understanding, and sent to New Jersey. It was not, however, from this Benjamin—a name still popular in the family—that the Virginia Wallers derive their origin. The first person of the name in Virginia was Edmund Waller, who bore the name of the poet, and was probably his grandson, and who came over in the beginning of the eighteenth century. His son Benjamin, the future judge, was born in 1716, was probably educated at William and Mary, and entered a clerk's office, in the duties of which he was profoundly versed. He was appointed clerk of the general court before the revolution, and attained to such distinction as a judge of law, that he was frequently consulted by the court, and is said to have given more opinions as chamber counsel, than all the lawyers of the colony united. He was appointed chief of three commissioners of admiralty under the republic, and as such was a member of the first court of appeals. It is said that his decisions were always sound law, but that he would never assign reasons for them. On the subject of the law of admiralty, his opinions were equally conclusive with the court and with clients. He died in 1786, at the age of 70. His influence, after the death of his daughter, on the mind of his grandson, will presently be seen.

Dorothea, the mother of our Littleton, was a lovely girl. Her name, which, from the ugly abbreviation of Dolly, has gone out of vogue, was popular with our fathers. It was borne by the brides of Patrick Henry, of James Madison, and of Henry Tazewell. It was honored in the strains of Spenser, in the sparkling prose of Sir Philip Sidney, and in the flowing verse of Waller; and finely shadows forth what a true woman ought to be and is—the gift of God. It was a favorite name in England, and evoked the sweetest measures of the poet Waller; and has ever been, probably from this circumstance, a family name among the Wallers of Virginia. A sweet portrait of Dorothea Waller, one of the finest productions of the elder Peale, always adorned the parlour of her distinguished son. In less than three years after the birth of Littleton, she died suddenly, and Mr. Tazewell had no recollection of his mother. It has often occurred to me that the true secret of the early retirement of Mr. Tazewell from the bar, might be found in the shortness of the lives of his progenitors. His grandfather Littleton died at the age of thirty-three, and his mother at the age of twenty-three; and when Mr. Tazewell retired from the bar, vigorous as he was, he was some years older than his father was at the time of his decease. It is believed that this same conviction was an element in that love of retirement which was the characteristic of Washington.

In a long, low wooden house, which may still be seen with its roof of red shingles, at the head of Woodpecker street, on the south side, in the city of Williamsburg, the residence of Judge Waller, and still owned by his grandson Dr. Robert Page Waller, and in a small room up stairs, at the north-east corner, looking on the street, in which his mother was born before him, on the seventeenth day of December, 1774, Littleton Waller Tazewell first saw the light. He was a healthy child, and, like all the children who were born about that time between the waters of the York and the James, was destined to frequent locomotion to avoid the marauding parties of the British, who for several years afterwards infested that region. As his mother died when he was in his third year, and as his father, who was engaged during the youth of Littleton in the Conventions, in the House of Delegates, or on the bench, was rarely at one place for any length of time, he lived, excepting a short interval in Greensville, with his grandfather Waller, who regarded with intense affection the beautiful orphan boy, preparing a trundle-bed for him in his own chamber, and watching him with parental solicitude. Until 1786 he lived with his grandfather, who taught him the rudiments of English and Latin, and superintended his studies at the school of Walker Murray; and when in that year the judge was on his death-bed, he sent for his old friend Mr. Wythe, and committed his grandson, then in his twelfth year, to his care; and with Mr. Wythe young Tazewell lived until that gentleman removed to Richmond, when he resided with Bishop Madison during his college course. The love which the child bore to his affectionate grandfather has been commemorated by a single fact. When Littleton came home from school and learned the old gentleman was dead, he was inconsolable, and finding that, in the painful anxieties of such a time, he was comparatively overlooked, he left the house, and went out into Col. Bassett's woods, where he had well-nigh perished. When he was missed, search was made for him, and he was found and brought home, but not until the funeral was over.

The following extract of a letter, addressed by Mr. Tazewell, in 1839, to William F. Wickham, Esq., the son and executor of the celebrated John Wickham of Richmond, and written on the death of that eminent lawyer, presents a sketch of his own early youth, not the less attractive as it embraces an interesting period of the youth of Mr. Wickham also :

" So much of my life," writes Mr. Tazewell, " was spent in the freest intercourse with your dear father, and during this intercourse mere time effected changes in our relations so gradually and imperceptibly, that, until they were matured into their last state, I was often at a loss to determine what was their true character. We first met in the year 1780, at the house of your grandfather, in Greensville county, (who was also the paternal grandfather of Mr. Tazewell), to which I had been sent to get me out of the way of the British army, then invading Virginia. I was a child not six years old, and he was a youth of about seventeen. Here he became my tutor ; and during the course of about two years, he taught me first to read English better than I could do before ; next, the rudiments of Latin, and lastly, to write. During this period I contracted for him that respect which children naturally feel for their seniors, and the ignorant for those much better informed than themselves ; while he regarded me with the affection usually bestowed by a patron upon his protegè, who manifests no bad propensities, and a disposition, at least, to profit by instruction and advice.

" In 1782 we parted ; and well do I remember the tears we both shed at our separation. In the winter of 1785–6 we again met at Williamsburg, at the house of my father, who then resided there. Here our intercourse was renewed upon a footing somewhat different than it had been maintained before, but with greater pleasure to both. He became a student of law in my father's office, and I was a boy in the first class of a celebrated grammar-school. To the careful instruction of my excellent grandfather* I had been indebted for greater proficiency in my classical learning than is usually acquired by boys of my time of life. My grandfather died within a very short period after the return of your

* Judge Benjamin Waller.

father to Virginia. Of the distress which I suffered at this deprivation, he was the sole comforter; and he immediately took upon himself the tasks which my poor old grandfather had been so delighted in performing for me. He heard and corrected my recitations—availed himself of every opportunity they offered to improve my taste and to inspire me with the wish of acquiring more information concerning the subjects to which they related. For all the pleasure which I have since derived from classical learning, I am indebted to his judicious instruction and advice.

"In 1787 your father commenced the practice of the law in Williamsburg, and mine shortly after removed from thence to Kingsmill, leaving me in Williamsburg under the care of your father to complete my education. Under his kind and useful advice, my rapid advance in my studies, both at school and in college, and my increased age, began to qualify me as a companion for him. By confiding to my discretion matters not often entrusted to those so young as I was, he taught me prudence; and, by his excellent precepts and example, he contributed much to the improvement of both my mind and manners."

As a boy of quick parts, Littleton doubtless observed with more or less attention the events that were passing around him. One proof of his recollection at an early age may be found in that shadowy notion which he carried to his grave, of the personal appearance of the venerable old treasurer, Robert Carter Nicholas, whom, as he died in 1780, he could only have seen when he was six years old. His father, as before observed, was constantly engaged in public life; and it is certain that young Tazewell had frequent opportunities of seeing the statesmen of that era. I well remember hearing him describe a visit he made to Patrick Henry, when the orator lived at Venable's Ford in Prince Edward, and his finding him in the shade of an oak playing the fiddle for the amusement of a group of girls and boys.

His first regular teacher was Walker Murray, with whom he prosecuted the study of Latin. At this school he began his intimacy with John Randolph. They were in the same class, and studied Cordery together; and here they formed a friendship which lasted without abatement until it was ended by the death of that eloquent but eccentric man. At parting—for Randolph went over to Bermuda—the young friends, who had no other property under their control, exchanged Corderys with each other; and nearly half a century afterwards, when one of them had become a Senator of the United States, and the other Minister Plenipotentiary to Russia, Randolph stated at a public dinner in Norfolk, that he still possessed the Cordery of Tazewell. I have heard Mr. Tazewell say that Randolph was very idle at school, that he was flogged regularly every Monday morning and two or three times during the week, and that he was the most beautiful boy at this period he ever beheld.

Young Tazewell at an early age entered the college of William and Mary, then under the presidency of Bishop Madison, and was, as may be presumed from his own statement, and as we learn from other sources, a diligent and accurate scholar. He was probably stimulated to exertion by the presence of several young men who were members of the institution at various times during his college course. Among these were James Barbour, of Orange, afterwards the colleague of Tazewell in the House of Delegates and in the Senate of the United States, Governor of Virginia, Secretary of War, and Minister to England, and renowned for his splendid eloquence and glowing patriotism; William Henry Cabell, also the colleague of Tazewell in the House of Delegates, Governor, and President of the Court of Appeals; George Keith Taylor, another colleague in the House of Delegates, a lawyer almost unrivalled at the bar, a patriot without fear and without reproach, who went down to an early grave; Robert Barraud Taylor, then in the flush of his brilliant youth, whom Tazewell was to meet at a memorable session on the floor of the House of Delegates, and who was to be his able and accomplished rival at the bar throughout his whole forensic career; John Randolph, and John Thompson.

Of John Thompson I have heard him say, in his latter years, that he was an extraordinary young man—the most wonderful he had ever seen. Thompson died young, at an age not exceeding twenty-three, and now lives only in the letters of Curtius. Mr. Tazewell always recounted in a tender tone his last interview with Thompson, who lived in Petersburg, but hearing that Tazewell was in Richmond, came over to see him, with a determination to return in the stage which left Richmond at twelve at night. He arrived at dusk, called on Tazewell, and told him that he had only from that time till midnight to talk with him; and in a few moments the friends were lost in pleasant converse. The night was dark and cold; and when the stage was announced, Thompson, who was thinly clad, bade his friend adieu. He took cold on his return, and died after a short illness.

Tazewell took the degree of Bachelor of Arts on the 31st day of July, 1792, though it is probable that he attended some of the classes at a later period. His diploma, written on a sheet of foolscap, and signed by Bishop Madison, Judge St. George Tucker, and others, is still preserved in his family. It speaks well for his attention and regularity, that of all his classmates he alone took a degree at the appointed time. Having finished his college course, he began the study of the law in Richmond under the auspices of Mr. Wickham,* living in his house as a member of his family, and of his father, who was then a Judge of the Circuit Court, but was soon after transferred to the Court of Appeals. That he entered with great zeal into the study of his profession, his subsequent familiarity with all the philosophy as well as the practice of the law fully shows. While engaged in the study, he regularly attended the courts of Richmond in which Wythe presided as sole chancellor, and Pendleton as the president of the Court of Appeals. The bar of the metropolis, which consisted mainly of men who had served during the Revolution, and subsequently, in camp and in council, was large in numbers and abounding in talents. Alexander Campbell, whose voice, says Wirt, "had all the softness and melody of the harp; whose mind was at once an orchard and a flower garden, loaded with the best fruits, and smiling in the many-colored bloom of spring; whose delivery, action, style, and manner, were perfectly Ciceronian," and who, I am grieved to say, was shortly to fall by his own hand; Munford, known to the profession by his Reports, and to scholars for the skill and elegance with which he has invested Homer in an English dress; Warden, the theme of many a joke, a sturdy lawyer of the old school, his name perpetually occurring in the early Reports; Call, whose aged form might occasionally be seen in Richmond in my early days, and

* Mr. Wickham married Mr. Tazewell's aunt, a half sister of Judge Henry Tazewell.

familiar by his Reports; Hay, afterwards a judge of the federal district court, which he held in this city thirty-five or forty years ago, but better known as the prosecuting attorney in the trial of Burr; and besides and above these were Edmund Randolph, who, having filled the most prominent posts in our own and in the federal government, and with whom it is believed Mr. Tazewell studied for a short time in Philadelphia, was to return to the bar, where he had the largest practice, according to Wirt, of any lawyer of his time; Wickham, then holding at or near his meridian as he did at his setting, the front rank; and John Marshall, a name that spoke for itself then, speaks for itself now, and will speak forever. These and such men composed the Richmond bar of that day.

An able bar is the best school of law. If the leaders be strong, they will be apt to have worthy successors; for of all lessons for a student, the contests of able men with each other in the practical game of life are the best. In such a school Tazewell applied himself closely; and in truth he had rare advantages. In a physical view he is said by one who knew him at this period of his life, to have been the most elegant and brilliant young man of his age. His tall stature, which reached six feet, his light and graceful figure, his blue, wide, intellectual eye, his features noble and prominent, though not yet developed to the sterner mould of latter years, those auburn ringlets, which curled about his head in childhood, which he shook at midnoon in the stress of some high argument, and which, turned to a silver hue, flowed down his marble neck in his shroud,—and a winning address, which, though slightly and insensibly tinged with hauteur on a first acquaintance, grew urgent and cordial, fascinated every beholder; while his intellectual faculties, which even thus early his habitual study of the severer sciences had sharpened, and which impelled him to venture fearlessly even with experts on vexed questions in law and morals, and his truly generous nature, made him the delight of the social circle, and endeared him to all. Then, as at a later day, he was not averse from manly sports, was fond of the gun, and was a fearless horseman. One of his youthful feats was to ride his horse to the second story of the Raleigh Tavern; and when his income from the Norfolk bar reached thousands, and his dicta were deemed the infallible utterances of Themis, he has been known in a country frolic to leap from a horse's back into a carriage in full motion; and at a later day, when the country sprang to arms to avenge the insult upon the Chesapeake, and he might have taken what civil or military post he pleased, he chose the command of a troop of cavalry. He understood at this early day, however, the art of sacrificing pleasure at the shrine of duty; and he preserved his youth pure from those flattering vices which please for the present, but which bring disgrace, disease, and death in their train.

His position gave him decided advantages of observation and improvement. His father, who was a prominent politician, and long a judge of the General Court, was now a judge of the Court of Appeals, and was soon elected to the Senate of the United States. In his society he saw Pendleton, Carrington, Roane, Fleming, and Lyons, who composed the Court of Appeals at that day, and all of whom I heard him recall in living colors a few months before his death. It was the custom of the judges of the Court of Appeals to put up at the Swan, where they might easily consult with Pendleton, their chief, whose injured limb prevented him for the last thirty years of his life from going abroad. It was at the Swan the judges kept their black cloth suits during the recess of the courts; for in those days there were no public conveyances; and all the judges, except Pendleton, who drove into Richmond from Caroline in a slow lumbering vehicle, nicknamed, after the wild driver of the coursers of the sun, a Phaeton, came into town on horseback, and were often clad in the cloth of their own looms. I mention these details of the early times of Mr. Tazewell, as they may serve to explain that stern simplicity of manners, of taste, and of general living, to which he resolutely adhered through life. Although fond of agriculture, and the owner of large landed estates, as he did not reside on them he did not require vehicles for the use of his family; and, at his residence in Norfolk, I think I may say that, for the last forty years at least, he never kept a carriage above the dignity of a gig, and I have doubts whether during that time he even kept a gig. The last time I saw him riding, some ten or twelve years ago, he was on horseback, accompanied by his son. I well remember when to take a drive in a carriage, or to use an umbrella, was deemed effeminate by some of the wealthiest planters in Virginia.

It was on the 14th day of May, 1796, that he received his license to practice law. The license, written in a bold hand on paper, was signed by judges Peter Lyons, Edmund Winston, and Joseph Jones, and is preserved by his children as a family relic. His first fee was derived from a warrant trying, in which a Mr. Taliaferro, who was his landlord, was a party, and was fifteen shillings, which helped to pay the rent of his office. His first important criminal case was the defence of a man on a charge of murder. Whether his client was innocent or guilty, I know not; but Tazewell got him clear of the law; and the man was so thankful for his services, that half a century afterwards he confessed his gratitude to a daughter of Mr. Tazewell, whom he chanced to see in the streets of a neighboring town.

The keen eye of John Marshall saw at once the caste of Tazewell's mind, and pronounced him an extraordinary young man. And I may say here, that the subdued manner and tone in which Mr. Tazewell spoke of Judge Marshall would convey a stronger impression of the character of the judge than any mere words of eulogy could well do. For his person and abilities he cherished the most profound respect and admiration. Even of the Life of Washington, which it was the fashion of the young democrats of my day to laugh at for the grammatical blunders and inverted English that marred the first edition of that work, Tazewell, who, though never eminent in elegant composition, always wrote good English, and saw all the faults of the work, still put a high value upon it as I certainly now do myself; and within a year of his death, when he was told an author was about to publish a history of the administration of Washington, he observed: "What can *he* tell that Judge Marshall has not told a great deal better already?" Yet, from the beginning of Mr. Tazewell's career to its close, they differed from each other on most of the great constitutional questions of their times. Candor compels me to say, however, that the decisions of the judge in the case of Maculloch against the Bank of Maryland, and in the case of Cohens against the State of Virginia, greatly disappointed him; and after their promulgation, though he still entertained feelings of high respect for his abilities, he would hardly have offered in honor of the judge that famous sentiment which he proposed at the Decatur dinner, and which elicited so much remark at the time.

But it was probably in his association with Chancellor Wythe, who loved and petted the promising boy, the son of his old neighbor in Williamsburg, whom he had taken from the dying bedside of another old neighbor, that Tazewell formed his taste for profound research, and his determination to master the law as a science. Wythe, above all our early statesmen, was deeply learned in the law, had traced all its doctrines to their fountain-heads, delighted in the year-books from doomsday down ; had Glanville, Bracton, Britton, and Fleta bound in collects ; had all the British statutes at full length, and was writing elaborate decisions every day, in which, to the amazement of county court lawyers, Horace and Aulus Gellius were sometimes quoted as authorities. And it is worthy of note, that Tazewell, affectionately attached as he was to Wythe, did not adopt his prejudices or antipathies, nor those peculiarities of punctuation and the disuse of capital letters at the beginning of sentences, which even Mr. Jefferson copied from his old master, but cherished a proper and becoming admiration for Pendleton, as will presently appear, between whom and Wythe there had been a life-long rivalry, and more recently some sharp judicial passages at arms, which we could wish were blotted out forever, but which, embodied in ever-during type, posterity must read and deplore. And, although he was in every material respect the architect of his own reputation, it has occurred to me that it was in memory of his affectionate relations with Wythe and Wickham, and with a view of paying the debt which he owed them, as well as from the natural goodness of his heart, that Tazewell was fond of the society of young men, and was ever ready to advise them in their studies, or to argue with them a difficult head in the law, and freely to assist them in other respects. An eminent counsel still living, though among the seniors of the Virginia bar, told me that once, when he was young, Mr. Tazewell, who had not opened a law book for years, explained to him the law respecting fine and recovery, and springing uses, so fully and with such ability as filled him with wonder ; and that his discourse, could it have been transferred to paper, would be an invaluable guide on that topic of the law. And many other young men have the same story to tell of his generous teachings on difficult questions. If all his personal attentions to the students of law were forgotten, the four letters which he prepared with infinite skill as a code of legal morals, and of the philosophical study of the law, would attest his sympathy and affection for his youthful friends.

While young Tazewell was gradually making his way at the bar, practising in James City, and in all the neighboring courts, he was called upon to take his stand in politics at one of the most tempestuous epochs in our annals. His father was one of that illustrious band of patriots, consisting of Patrick Henry, George Mason, William Grayson, Richard Henry Lee, Benjamin Harrison, John Tyler, and others, who believed that the General Federal Convention, which had been summoned merely to amend the Articles of Confederation, had exceeded their powers in framing an entirely new instrument, the present federal constitution, and they warmly opposed its ratification by Virginia. When the new system was adopted, they watched its operations with a jealous eye, and opposed some of the leading measures of the administration of Washington. When it was foreseen that a new treaty would be negotiated with England, it was determined by them that, unless that measure made those concessions and amendments of the treaty of 1783, which Virginia had striven so hard to obtain, it should be opposed at every hazard; and John Taylor of Caroline, happening to resign his seat in the Senate just at that time (1795), Henry Tazewell, then on the bench of the Court of Appeals, was elected to fill his place; and the first movement he made on taking his seat in the Senate was to offer a series of resolutions pointing out the defects of the new treaty with England, which had been negotiated by Mr. Jay. It was natural that young Tazewell should embrace the doctrines of the party in which his father held almost the chief place; and his inclination in this respect was probably strengthened by the opinions of Judge Pendleton and Chancellor Wythe, both of whom had voted for the ratification of the federal constitution by Virginia, but who now sided with his father. On the other hand, his friends Marshall and Wickham were ranged on the federal side; and though Wickham at no time of his life took an active part in politics, Marshall, in the House of Delegates, and by popular addresses, was most active in the cause, and was reputed the leader of the federal party in the State.

In the spring of 1796, when he had attained his one-and-twentieth year, he was returned to the House of Delegates from the county of James City, and continued a member of the body until the close of the century. In that interval were discussed in the Assembly the leading measures of the administrations of Washington and the elder Adams; and a better school for a young politician cannot well be imagined. Of this period, the most interesting sessions were those of 1798–99, and of 1799–1800. During the first of these sessions, the famous resolutions of John Taylor of Caroline, which, it afterwards transpired, were drafted by Mr. Madison, were discussed with an ability which was honorable to both the great parties of the day, and which, at this distance of time, is proudly remembered; and in the last-named session was adopted that still more celebrated paper, from the pen of Madison, now known and honored as the Virginia Report. To both of these important papers Tazewell gave a cordial assent. It was during these two sessions he met with several of his college mates, as well as with some older statesmen whom he had not before seen in a public body. Among those who adhered to his side of the question were James Barbour, of Orange, the late Judge Daniel, of the General Court, one of the keenest minds of his time, the late Judge Cabell, president of the Court of Appeals, Wilson Cary Nicholas, afterwards Senator and Governor, Judge Archibald Stuart, Chancellor Creed Taylor, Governor Giles, Thomas Newton, Governor Plea ants, Samuel Tyler, French Strother, and Mr. Madison; and among those of the opposite side, were George Keith Taylor, his eloquent namesake from Norfolk, Robert Barraud Taylor, the late venerable John Eyre, Thomas M. Bayly, John Wise, James Breckenridge, Archibald Magill, and Henry Lee, of the Legion.

A painful domestic incident happened at this time, which had a material influence upon the future plans of Mr. Tazewell. Having lost his mother in his third year, he may be said hardly to have known a mother's love; and he had fixed his affections on his elegant and accomplished father, who was his senior by only one and twenty years, who was in the vigor of manhood, and before whom a long and splendid career seemed to be in reserve. But this pleasing hope was destined to perish. Judge Tazewell, on his journey to Philadelphia, where Congress then held its sittings, had taken a severe cold, but was able to reach the city, and on the 21st day of

January, 1799, took his seat in the Senate. He was then evidently ill; and on the 24th, three days after, breathed his last. Thus, at the age of 45, died Henry Tazewell, when his fame to human eyes had not reached the zenith; when, though still in the full strength of manhood, he had received more and higher political and judicial honors than Virginia had ever before conferred on one so young; when, having been twice elected president of the Senate, at a time when that honor was deemed only second to that of the presidency of the United States, he stood above his Virginia competitors, with only one illustrious exception, on the lists of fame, and when the expiration of a few months would have placed his only son in Congress by his side.

While the politics of the stormy period of 1800 were at the height, Gen. Marshall, as the since illustrious Chief Justice was then called, having accepted from Mr. Adams an invitation to the department of State, vacated his seat in the House of Representatives; and young Tazewell, then in his twenty-sixth year, and younger than John Randolph was when the orator first took his seat, was elected by an overwhelming majority, over Col. Mayo, the federal candidate, in his place, and made his appearance in the House on the 26th day of November, 1800. Of Mr. Tazewell's short term of service in Congress, I shall pass over all details in this rapid sketch, except to remark that he was present at that fearful contest in the House of Representatives, when a deliberate effort was made by the federal party to elect a man as president of the United States, who had not received a single vote in the electoral colleges for that office, over Jefferson, who had received a plurality of votes for president. The painful excitement of that scene, which lasted continuously day and night, and during which sick members were brought in beds to the House and kept there, Tazewell never forgot; nor do I think the events of that day made a favorable impression on his mind of the morals of politics. That he, who was a republican, should have been elected so easily the successor of Gen. Marshall, who had been elected recently over a democratic opponent, shows how much, even in the highest party times, the influence of individual character is felt by the people. I need not say that Tazewell voted for Mr. Jefferson. At the close of his term in 1801, he returned home, withdrew from public life, and made his preparations to take up his abode in Norfolk. At this time he was universally regarded by his political friends as the first young man in the State, and the most dazzling honors which a victorious party could confer upon him, seemed to be within his reach. How he fulfilled the expectations of his party, will presently appear.

When asked in his latter years by a friend who knew his aversion to the ordinary routine of legislative life, and his devotion to the business of his clients, what induced him to enter the House of Delegates so young, and continue in it so long, he said: "*My father made me:*" a saying characteristic of Mr. Tazewell, who never put any value upon his own services, and must be taken with many grains of allowance; for, although it could not be otherwise than grateful to the feelings of a father who was a senator of the United States, and in many ways agreeable at that perilous epoch to have such a representative in the Assembly, yet we must count much on that love of distinction which glows so warmly in the finest minds, and which Tazewell certainly felt at times, and continued to feel as long as he lived; and his father knew, from his own experience and success at the bar, that a year or two in the popular branch of the Assembly is no mean preparation for active business, and especially for the pursuits of the forum. It was in the same spirit, when, visited by the greatest living statesman of New England, that sterling patriot, and that peerless orator of his whole country, Edward Everett, who, seeing the faculties of Mr. Tazewell still vigorous in his 85th year, expressed to him his regret that he had retired from public life so early, he replied: "*I'm only sorry that I ever entered it at all;*" when all who knew Mr. Tazewell intimately can avouch that, even at that moment of his 85th year, if the State of Virginia had called upon him to defend her right or honor in any transaction which may have occurred from the settlement of Jamestown to the late Ohio boundary discussion, he would have had every mouldering record from the office of the General Court, and every book bearing upon the subject, clustering in heaps around him in less than sixty hours after he had undertaken his task.

It was in 1802 that Mr. Tazewell, who had qualified as an attorney in the Hustings Court of the Borough on the 26th day of June of the previous year, took up his abode in Norfolk. Whoever would form an opinion of the Norfolk of 1802 from the Norfolk of 1860, would be apt to fall into many and capital mistakes. As you entered the harbor of that day, many sloops, schooners, brigs, barques, and ships obstructed your way ; and you would see the wharves and the warehouses, such as they were, in full employment. A number of small houses, which were used as retail shops, sailor-boarding establishments, and for other purposes, lined Broadwater, which was then not much more than half as long as it is now, and Little Water, nearly their western length. Market square, the houses of which were almost wholly wood, and mean and contemptible in appearance, was the home of the wholesale and more respectable retail dealers in dry goods and hardware. The larger grocery dealers centred near the then head of Broadwater. The population ranged between 6,500 and 7,500, and consisted of a large infusion of French from the West India islands, Scotch and English in considerable proportions, Irish, and New English. There were some Dutch, Spanish, and Portuguese. Our Norfolk born people, and the people from the neighboring counties, formed the base—a pretty broad base, but only a base. Everybody was busy. Wirt, writing a year or two later to a friend, likened the borough to a hive in which their was no drone. The outward appearance of things was bad enough. The houses on the wharves and in the business streets were all of wood, and have since been swept away by successive fires. There was not a paved street within the bills of mortality. Immense pools of mud and water were seen everywhere ; and it was a favorite amusement of the boys to watch the attempt of a loaded dray to pass through those beds of muck. There were three merchants at farthest, whose wealth, on a most liberal estimate, might possibly average $100,000, though they thought themselves worth a good deal more. There was but one brick church, and that was the present St. Paul's, not, as we now see it, with its tasteful interior, but a rude brickkiln with an enormous cocked hat stuck upon it. The people heard preaching in the upper rooms of warehouses, in the courthouse, or in some rickety concern knocked up for the nonce. The clergy fared badly. The rector of a large brick church, then rising, with a wealthy congregation, received for his services one hundred pounds, Virginia currency, which equal three hundred and thirty-three dollars and thirty-three cents of our money, and both pastor and people seemed to be satisfied with the bargain. Small houses, some of which may still be seen, straggled out along Church street, to what is now called Fort Barbour, though not so called till twelve years later. There was hardly an elegant private residence in the city. The bricks, of which the best houses were built, were rough and roughly laid. The houses had no conveniences, except here and there a closet. They were, however, substantially built, and were neatly finished within. They invariably had one thing which is fast passing away. There was the smoke-house in which every housekeeper cured his meat; and there was the dairy; but how they could put the dairy to its proper use I could never find out. The people had cows, and the cows gave milk; but there was no running water, and there was no ice. Long years passed before ice was introduced. The gentlemen of the bar were awake, and made out very well—much better than the clergy. The very youngest of the profession fed freely and voluptuously on the black eyes and cracked crowns of Little Water street, with an occasional haul from Exchange alley and the river Styx. A set, rather older, ventured into the expanse of Broadwater, and talked of the relations of landlord and tenant, of master and apprentice, and sometimes, in that belligerent neighborhood, of husband and wife, and not unfrequently of the writ of breaking the close. But the main harvest of the bar was from the shipping and from commerce, the daughter of the sea, which was soon to be vexed by the imperial decrees and orders in council of foreign powers, and by some retaliatory legislation of our own. The highest standard of remuneration for the services of lawyers was what we would now deem low. Wirt, writing from Norfolk in 1805, considered two thousand dollars to be laid up at the end of the year a fair reward for the highest talents. One of the ablest leaders of the bar declared, seven years later, that when he was worth fifty thousand dollars he would retire from practice; while Wirt declared that he would retire as soon as he had accumulated a capital which would yield the annual interest of four thousand dollars. It is certain that all the members of the bar of that day, as did all of the merchants, died poor with two prominent exceptions; and when we reflect that those two men held the front rank at the bar, one of them at least twenty years, the other near thirty, and neither on his withdrawal could be deemed wealthy, the inference is irresistible that, though now and then in that interval a big fee came rolling in from some vessel caught in the act of violating the embargo, or, at a much later date, from some prize case in the war between Spain and her South American colonies, the rewards of legal merit were low.

There was a branch of the old Bank of the United States, whose entire capital, distributed over the Union, was only ten millions. There was as yet, and fourteen years later, no daily paper. The *Herald*, then in its ninth year, was published three times a week, and was the organ of the democratic party. It was not until two years later that the *Ledger* appeared in the field, under the lead of that able champion John Cowper, and gave the federal flag to the breeze. More than fourteen years were to elapse before a daily paper was established. The equinoctial storms sadly worried our fathers. From the imperfect filling in of the streets and wharves, the tides rose high; and then, if we would keep out of sight St. Mark's, the Rialto, and the palaces of merchant princes, Norfolk was another edition of Venice. The canoe was our gondola, and "*yo heave oh*" were our echoes of Tasso. A bold stream, that would float a vessel of one hundred tons, cut Granby and Bank streets in two, and just halted on the west side of Church, where it was almost met by another furious stream from Newton's Creek. At Town Bridge a torrent raged that was not to be crossed until the tide fell. Freemason, between Brewer and Granby, presented a sea deep enough to float a vessel of one hundred tons. Our Rialto on Granby was not erected till eighteen or twenty years later; and I remember our fathers were so proud of it, that they invited strangers to see it. It took, for a time, the shine from the Navy Yard. The health of the town ranked the lowest. The tombstones in old St. Paul's tell of the number of captains of vessels and trading merchants who died here. The letters of Wirt show the prevalent belief that an acclimating process was just as necessary here as at New Orleans and Havana, or on the coast of Africa. It was the fear of yellow fever, perpetually dinned in his ears by his country friends, who but echoed the popular belief, that drove Wirt away. Such was Norfolk, not enveloped in the mists of tradition, but such as she was, when Mr. Tazewell came to reside here in 1802.

He lived to behold a very different state of things. He lived to see it one of the cleanest cities in the world, and to see more miles of paved streets in Norfolk than any other city south of the Potomac can boast of; and those streets lighted up every night with a brilliancy equal to that which a rejoicing people, thirteen years later than 1802, kindled in commemoration of the victory of New Orleans, and of the peace with Great Britain. He lived to see the Negro population as well clad, and the female part of it as fully crinolined, as the great body of the respectable white people of 1802, and worshipping every Sabbath in churches of their own, better and more costly than the best church of that day; while the white people have added, and are adding every day, church to church and chapel to chapel, some of which are even elegant in their architecture, and all comfortable in their arrangements beyond the conceptions of that day. He lived to see, instead of three men worth one hundred thousand each, three men, one of whom he was, whose united wealth would reach a million, besides many others with one hundred thousand down to ten thousand. He lived to see the population increased from seven thousand to seventeen thousand; and, to say the least, fully as well clad, as well fed, as their fathers ever were, and living in better houses than their fathers ever lived in. He lived to see our banking capital, whether invested in public banks, in savings institutions, and in the hands of private bankers, swell above the fragmentary portion which the old Bank of the United States could afford to allot to us, to somewhat over two millions of dollars, almost wholly owned by our own people; and to read our monthly bills of mortality, which attest, beyond the reach of cavil, a condition of general health without a parallel in the annals of cities laved by the tides. He lived to see the farmers, who supplied the population of 1802 with vegetables and fish enough to serve, but none to spare, ship off nearly half a million's worth to the north every season; and to see land in the neighborhood, which in 1802 was worth hardly anything more than what the doctor reaped from its crop of agues, become salubrious, and sell for fifty dollars an acre. He lived to see our city connected with the West, the South, and the North, by steamships whose tonnage would in those days have been pronounced fabulous, by railways, and by the magnetic telegraph. He lived to see a larger tonnage arriving and departing annually from our port than ever was seen in our most prosperous days. The old figure of trade has, indeed, passed away ; and some wharf owners, some warehouse men, and some others do not reap the profits of old times, though, by the way, we now have more and better wharves, more and better warehouses, than they had at that day ; and the cause and the necessity of the change are obvious. The trade of our fathers in 1802 was an unnatural trade. It was a fungus that sprung from the diseased condition of foreign powers. It was not the result of developed productive wealth, but the accident of the war between the two greatest commercial nations of the globe, which gave us the carrying trade. It was born of other people's troubles, and destined to die when those troubles were appeased. It may be safely affirmed, that the business of Norfolk, the natural result of enterprise, progress, and development, and not the offspring of foreign action, at Mr. Tazewell's death, exceeded, in a large degree, the business of Norfolk in 1802, puffed up, as it was, by ephemeral causes, and that the present wealth of our people immeasurably surpasses the wealth of the past.

Whatever may have been the rate of legal compensation in 1802, some description of the leading members of the bar of that day is indispensable to the canvas, of which Mr. Tazewell is the principal figure. Besides Hyott, who lived in the retired mansion in which our venerable fellow-citizen, John Southgate, now resides, and whose name has long been extinct, and Marsh, who studied in the famous law school of Judge Reeves, at Lichfield, where Calhoun was initiated in the mysteries of the law, who built that handsome wooden house in the fields, long since burned down, in which the youth of my day were flogged through the rudiments of Ruddiman, and whose sons are among the enterprising merchants and sea-captains of our modern city, was, first and foremost, General THOMAS MATHEWS. There he stands, with the figure of Apollo and with the spirit of Mars, clad in the blue and buff of the revolution, wearing that sword which he had worn through the struggle with the mother country, his well-powdered head surmounted by the old cocked hat which he had worn when driven from Fort Nelson by the myrmidons of his British namesake, and at the siege of York, and with that long queue, the dressing of which was the no mean labor of the toilet of that era. To his dying day, which happened on the eve of the late war with Great Britain, though a general of brigade, on all stated musters he appeared in the field in full uniform, and was greeted by old and young with applause. He was a native of St. Kitts, left the island before the revolution, performed his part gallantly through the entire contest for independence, and had long been a member of the House of Delegates, of which he was again and again elected speaker, performing the duties of the chair with a dignity, firmness, and grace still freshly remembered, and bequeathing his name to a beautiful county overlooking the waters of the Chesapeake, which it still bears. He served in the assembly at a memorable period. The questions of the age were to be settled. He recorded his name in favor of the bill establishing religious freedom, where it will shine for ever. He voted for the resolution convoking the meeting at Annapolis, which was the seminal germ of the present federal constitution. He voted to send delegates to the Federal Convention, which formed the present federal constitution; and in the convention which ratified that instrument in the name of Virginia, he voted for its adoption; and when Norfolk commemorated the installation of the federal constitution by the firing of guns, by the display of flags, by civic, mechanical, and military processions, conspicuous on that great day was the general, who acted as the Chief Priest of the august ceremonies which honored the birth of a nation. He was always elected to any office to which the people could call him. His address had the tinge of the soldier, but was most fascinating. No familiarity could impair its effect. The bar regarded him with affection and reverence. All the men about town loved him. The women almost adored him. A smile from the General on a gala-day, when mounted on his charger, which he managed well to the last, or the lifting of his three-cornered hat on the sidewalk, was a trophy which the prettiest woman, maid or matron, would treasure away among the *spolia opima* of her hoard. His social position was of the highest. He was known far and wide, and played most becomingly the part of host to distinguished persons from abroad. Some of our old citizens remember the coaches and four which used to pass down King's lane to his modest residence at the foot of tide. One of the acts of his life was characteristic. He was on a visit to his brother at St. Kitts, when the French fleet lay-to off the island, and levied a sum of money upon the people, which they paid. The French then levied another sum, which the people of the island were wholly unable to pay. In this dilemma the people of St. Kitts had recourse to General Mathews, who, dressed in his uniform as an American general officer, went on board the hostile fleet, and induced the admiral to accept an order from him on the American Consul in Paris, for the sum in question. The fleet then sailed away, and the island was safe. In due time the order came back protested. Suit was brought and judgment obtained against him, and the venerable patriot spent his last days in prison bounds for a debt which the British Government ought to have paid with gratitude as well as with money. In 1802 he was approaching his sixtieth year, but was vigorous and attentive to business. He was a fine speaker. His voice was melodious, and its compass exceeded belief. It could be heard along the line of a whole brigade, and in the clatter of a skirmish. It is one of the traditions of the bar, that he could, by condensing his voice as he approached it, break a pane of glass in pieces. His learning was respectable; and with the jury he had great weight; and he was heard with respect by the court; and always having lived and practised in sea-ports, he had no inconsiderable knowledge of the law of admiralty. In the Chesapeake war, old as he was, his spirit fired up. He took command as brigadier, and longed for another crack at the British. His descendants still survive, and one of them holds an important federal office in our modern city. With all the demonstrations of public grief, his remains were committed to the grave in the south-east angle of the yard of St. Paul's.

Another leader of the bar was the venerable JAMES NIMMO. His tall form, neatly attired in black, and bent low as in grateful obeisance to the rapid years which were bringing him nearer to his heavenly home; that broad belt of baldness that stretched over from his forehead to his spine, those silver side-locks that ran wild about his collar, that honest, peculiar voice, which sounded as if virtue and piety, descending awhile from the upper sphere, were helping the old man out in his speech ; with the freshness of yesterday I see and hear them all. Though seemingly attended by celestial visitants, and perhaps for that reason, he had not a particle of Young America about him. He believed that rogues and scamps ought to be punished as promptly and as condignly now as in the days of Abraham, of Isaac, and of Jacob, and as in the days of his own early youth ; and while he was the aid and comforter of the widow and the fatherless, and of the virtuous poor,—would weep and pray with them, and help them out of that slim purse, which never held an unworthy shilling, he was, as Commonwealth's attorney, the terror of evil-doers. I remember on one occasion, when he was prosecuting a notorious offender whom he sent to the penitentiary, and who was defended by Gen. Taylor, as the old man was bald, and the air of the old court-house was damp, he threw over his head a red bandanna handkerchief, and I hear the laugh which Gen. Taylor extorted from the bench, from the jury, and from the old man himself, by calling it a bloody flag. He was of that substantial class of lawyers, who, having received an elementary grounding in Latin and mathematics in the schools of the time, entered the clerk's office, and served a term of duty within its precincts. He was thus well versed in the ordinary forms of the law, and with the decisions of the courts in leading cases ; and took the hue rather of an attorney than of an advocate. With such men as a class, there was no great intimacy with the law as a science, and its higher philosophy was beyond their reach. Like Mathews, however, he had always lived in sea-ports, and as he studied his cases well, he was always very impressive with the jury, and was heard with great respect by the court ; and when he had reached the zenith, a slow shake of the head or even of his finger at an argument that was too hard for him, went a great way even with the court, and almost all the way with the jury. As long as the case lay in the old routine, this class of lawyers would get along very well ; but novelties were unpleasant to them ; they hated the subtleties of special pleading ; and they turned pale at a demurrer. Possessed of a high spirit, which sometimes, even beyond threescore, sent forth a flash as vivid as it was sudden, he was placable and ever prompt to make an atonement. He was now in his forty-eighth year, and in the full vigor of a temperate middle life ;

but he lived to be the father of the bar for almost the third of a century, and almost to be the father of the town, which in an honorable sense he was ; dying in January, 1833, at the age of seventy-eight, and laid away by the hands of descendants among patrimonial graves at Shenstone Green. He was a true patriot. In the hour of her fiercest trial he stood by the side of Virginia. While so many men of wealth and influence in the neighboring counties of Princess Anne and Norfolk, impelled by their fears, present and prospective, of British power, and living within the range of British guns, faltered in their faith to the young republic, and took British protection, Nimmo clung to the standard of his country; and, having been taken prisoner, was confined on board the Liverpool frigate when she fired the shot which, striking the south-eastern angle of St. Paul's Church, has left its mark for posterity. One recollection personal to myself shows this fine old man in an amiable view. I had received, at the age of one-and-twenty, an important trust from the people of Norfolk ; and Mr. Nimmo, meeting me in the street the morning after the election, and taking in his own pure hands both of mine, said : " My young friend, remember that you owe a double service—service to your God as well as to your country ; and that he who is faithless to the God of his fathers can never be faithful to his country." And now, when the day of ambition with me is long past and gone, and when that day of retribution, which, as it cometh to all, so it shall come to us, is drawing nigh, I may say that it ever has been my fervent and steadfast prayer to be able to illustrate in my humble life the precept of my pious friend.

There was another lawyer, the junior of Nimmo by five years, whose subsequent intimate connexion with Mr. Tazewell makes it proper to recall his position here. The name of Col. JOHN NIVISON was pronounced with pride by our fathers, and deserves to be held in grateful remembrance. None under seventy can recall him as he pleaded at the bar ; and none under fifty, and very few of that age, can recall him as he sat in the chair of the Recorder. That office was justly held in high repute in olden time. Sir John Randolph held it ; and at a later day it was held by the celebrated Edmund Randolph, the great grandson of the knight, and by the eloquent and accomplished Henry Tazewell. Then it was usually bestowed upon some prominent lawyer who had retired from the bar, and within my recollection it has ever been held by upright, intelligent, and honorable men. I see this old man, too, with the freshness of the passing hour, as he was driving out in his capacious chariot to Lawson's, or as he strolled or rather rocked along the sidewalk. He was very large, weighing between two and three hundred, and was nearly six feet in height. He said he had no idea of his bulk until, passing a negro woman in the street with a basket on her head who took a side glance at him, he heard her unconsciously exclaim : " Good gracious, what a big white man!" He was born in 1760, in Brunswick as Brunswick then was, was educated at William and Mary, while Wythe was professor of law, having as his college associates John Marshall, Spencer Roane, the amiable and patriotic Samuel Hardy, who was destined to fall too soon, and at whose grave Virginia sat in mourning, Archibald Stuart, Bushrod Washington, William Short, our Minister to Spain, *et alii haud impares:* was one of the founders of the Phi Beta Kappa Society—an institution which will make his name immortal—and began the practice of the law in his native county. After the peace of 1783, he took up his abode in Portsmouth, where he reached the head of the bar ; and in the great hegira from that town on the adoption of the federal constitution in 1788, he came over to Norfolk, where he had now long held the front rank in his profession. He too had passed a noviciate in the Clerk's office, had studied law under the guidance of Wythe, and had been very successful. Like Nimmo, he was called the honest lawyer ; and it was one of the sly jests of our fathers that there should be two lawyers at the same bar and in the same generation, whose claims to the title should be generally conceded by the people. In 1802 he had reached his forty-second year ; and having acquired a competent fortune—for moderation was the order of those times—he was soon to withdraw from the bar, and to fill the chair of the Recorder. He is said to have been very successful in making lawyers eloquent and entertaining while he was on the bench. Whether he was fond of the classics, I cannot affirm ; but he certainly borrowed a trait from Homer, and nodded occasionally ; and when a tedious speaker began his harangue, having already taken a full view of the law and facts of the case, he usually fell asleep, waking up as the counsel finished his harangue, much refreshed at least, if not instructed by it, and proceeded to give judgment in the case. He was noted for his tenderness to the poor, and it is said that he had on their account almost as much business after he withdrew from the bar as before. He died in 1820, at the age of sixty, and was buried in St. Paul's, within a few feet of his compatriot Mathews. When Col. Nivison, in December, 1776, was returning to his lodgings after organizing the Phi Beta Kappa Society, he might have seen a pretty infant of two years in the nurse's arms, or toddling in the shade of Waller's grove ; but he could not have foreseen that the same little fellow would in the course of time worry him with all the art of the special pleader, and finally receive from him the hand of his eldest daughter ; and that when he should withdraw from the bar, he was to leave all his business in the hands of that child.

But there was a young man, a member of the bar in 1802, whose elegant person, whose winning address, whose uncommon abilities, which were associated with industry and perseverance quite as uncommon, and whose glowing patriotism, would have made an impression in any country and in any age, and gained distinction in any sphere. Under such a portrait the name of one man only can be written—that of Robert Barraud Taylor. Young Taylor was eleven months older than Tazewell, was born in Smithfield, attended in Norfolk the school of that elegant scholar, the late Dr. Alexander Whitehead, became a student of William and Mary College, where he remained till his duel with John Randolph, in which he received a ball that he carried to his grave ; studied law with Judge Marshall, and in 1796, at the age of twenty-two, engaged in the practice of the law in this city. His fine talents attracted universal attention, and business crowded upon him. His voice, action, eloquence, were all in fine harmony. As the district court system was then in operation, he had an opportunity of witnessing the displays of the leading counsel of the state in the neighboring town of Suffolk ; and it was the dictate alike of interest and ambition to prepare himself for the conflict with his ablest contemporaries. Politics were the order of the day ; and they soon engaged the attention of young Taylor. I heard many years ago, that when he came to the bar, and some time afterwards, he sided with his college mates Tazewell, Randolph, Cabell, Thompson, and James Barbour, and hailed with rapture the progress of the French revolution ; but, shocked by the barbarities which disgraced the later stages of that moral and political maelstrom, and indignant at the unprecedented conduct of the diplomatic agents of France in our own country, he determined to separate from his early friends, and to uphold with all his influence the administration of Washington and that of his successor. It is said that he read with unmixed feelings of admiration and delight the Reflections of Burke on the French Revolution, which had appeared about six years before ; and, if that work vanquished his early love of France, he may be said at least to have fallen by a noble hand. At such a crisis of foreign and domestic affairs, it was impossible that a young man with such powers of eloquence and such fearlessness of spirit should be allowed to remain at home, while all his old associates, and the oldest and ablest politicians of the state were about to assemble in Richmond, and to battle for the victory. He was accordingly returned, in 1799, by the Borough of Norfolk to the House of Delegates, on the floor of which the contest was to be decided. At the session of the previous year, the Assembly had passed the celebrated resolutions of John Taylor of Caroline, long since known to have been written by Mr. Madison, which had been sent to the several states. The leading object of the present session was to refer the answers of the states to a committee, and to report an argument in defence of the resolutions of the previous year. The report, since so well known as the Report of '99, or the Virginia Report, drawn by Madison, was the consequence. When it was presented to the House of Delegates, it was discussed by the prominent men of both parties with eminent ability. Young Taylor performed his part with his usual zeal and force, and, by the side of his illustrious namesake, George Keith Taylor, opposed the adoption of the Report, which prevailed, however, by a decided majority. He also sustained Mr. Adams for the presidency in preference to Mr. Jefferson ; and, when Mr. Jefferson was elected, he opposed his administration up to 1802, when Tazewell came to reside in Norfolk. Though opposed then, and as long as he lived, to the party which, with few and short intermissions, has controlled, from 1789 to the present day, the political action of the state, his devotion to our blessed mother was as pure and as ardent as was ever felt by any son who drew nurture from her bosom ; and he was as prompt to avenge her wrongs as to assert her rights—at once a D'Aguessau in the forum and a Bayard in the field. Nor was that affection unreturned. When the clouds of war were gathering round her, Virginia entrusted her safety and her honor to his sword; and when the returning light of peace shone upon her hills and valleys and over the green savannahs of the East, and he had withdrawn from the arena of his splendid fame, she invested him with her ermine, which he wore with becoming grace to his dying hour; and she stood in tears at his tomb.

In this young man, Tazewell was to find an intimate friend, a fit, an able, and a lifelong competitor. They were nearly of the same age: they had been classmates in College, and had been in the Assembly together; and while Tazewell was studying law in Mr. Wickham's office in Richmond, Taylor was following suit a few doors off in the office of Gen. Marshall. Even on the score of physical beauty they were not unmatched. Though belonging to different models, each in his sphere was, in youth, in middle life, and in old age, among the finest looking men of their generation. Sometimes the aspect of Taylor was magnificent. I saw him one afternoon thirty years ago as he was returning from the court in Portsmouth. He was passing from Toy and King's corner to Hall's. The waves of recent debate were sweltering in his breast. His person was erect; his gait was rapid; with one hand he held his cloak in a graceful fold, and with the other he grasped his ivory curule staff. I thought of Cicero hastening up the Capitoline hill to announce in the forum the death of Catiline on the Picenian plain and the slaughter of the traitor's band.

There were, however, some differences between them, which, or some of which, observable at first, grew more distinct in the lapse of years, in their places of nativity, in their temperaments, in their intellectual traits, and in their politics. Both were partly of Gallic descent; but here they differed as in other things. Tazewell was French on the father's side; Taylor on the mother's. Tazewell's ancestors were from that city on the banks of the Seine in which the piratical Northmen had dwelt, which they had made the capital of a warlike empire extorted from one of the drivelling descendants of Charlemagne, and which they had called by the defiant title of Normandy. Taylor's ancestors belonged to that pious and not less heroic race, which, under the name of Huguenots, battled, not for rapine and conquest, but for the rights of conscience and for a large public liberty, and which, though defeated and driven from their ancestral land, the beautiful land of the fig, the olive, and the vine, to the chalky shores of old England, were more than triumphant in the virtue of their cause. The music familiar to the ears of Tazewell's ancestors was the wind from the boisterous North Sea and the turbulent Bay of Biscay; while Taylor's forefathers were refreshed by the gentle gales of Araby blown across the blue Mediterranean to the banks of the Rhone. The blood of both had been strongly mixed with the blood of that Anglo-Saxon race, which, crushed at times, and even for centuries, was apt to rise again, and build its fortresses to freedom out of the ruins of the very temples of its oppressors.

Tazewell was born on the north side of the James, Taylor on the south—a distinction of no little significance in Virginia politics to this very hour. Tazewell, insensibly imitating those grave old rovers of the sea whom he counted among his kin, was, even under great provocation, cool and wary, and only the more dangerous; Taylor, whose southern blood coursed in torrents of fire through his veins, though at times in the highest degree self-poised and calm, had less command of his temper, and showed more plainly the smart of the hostile shaft; and, though prompt as lightning to return it, did not always send it back to the enemy as steadily as he might have done with more deliberation. Their modes of reasoning differed as widely as their temperaments. Each was a supreme master of reasoning in his respective department; and, if we look along their entire course at the bar, it is hard to say which of the two won the most verdicts. Perhaps, though both of these able men wielded at times an almost omnipotent sway over juries and over the bench; yet it may be said that the style of Tazewell was more decisive with the court, and that of Taylor with the jury. Each seemed necessary to the greatness of the other; and it is probable that, if Tazewell had not been constantly pressed throughout his career by such a man as Taylor, he would never have made those wonderful displays before a jury and in popular assemblies which form no small part of his fame; and that Taylor, unless checked by the severe logic of Tazewell, would, indeed, have been, as he was, the great advocate of his time, but would have failed to acquire that reputation for profound ability and learning in the law, which no less a judge than Marshall acknowledged in terms of high commendation. In a strictly legal point of view, it would have been best that both these able men had been removed in early life from the deteriorating influence of inferior courts, and transferred to a higher sphere. Had they gone together to New York, and had been compelled to follow their cases through the highest courts as well as the lowest, or had confined themselves to appellate tribunals, they would in their daily efforts have reared a legal reputation coextensive with the Union, and, perhaps, more durable. It is only necessary to state that Taylor remained at the bar ten years after the retirement of Tazewell; that he was then called upon to preside in the courts in which he had reaped his brilliant fame; that, when a long and honored judicial career seemed to stretch before him, he was snatched away at the comparatively early age of sixty; and that Tazewell survived him more than a quarter of a century.*

Before we leave the Court-room of 1802, glancing, as we pass, at the face of young Maxwell, then just returned from Yale, who four years later was to make a name for himself, and of Arthur and Richard Henry Lee, brothers, whose sparkling eloquence ruled the fierce democracy of the day, and bespoke its ancestral source, and of others who were about to step on the threshold of professional life, the young man, sitting at the clerk's table, and intent upon his work, raising now and then his dark chestnut eyes to the Counsel or to the Court, his jet black hair curling about his tall forehead, his erect port telling of the military exercises in which he so much delighted and excelled, seems, in vision, to rise before me. Born in Henrico, within a stone's throw of the birthplace of Henry Clay, who was his intimate personal friend and colleague in the clerk's office under Peter Tinsley,—the countyman and colleague also of our late esteemed fellow-citizen, Thomas Williamson, another pupil of Tinsley,—he had performed such faithful service in the General Court, that at the age of twenty-

* For a sketch of Mr. Tazewell and Gen. Taylor, as they appeared at this early period of their career, see the graphic picture drawn by the hand of Mr. Wirt, in the Old Bachelor, Appendix No. 3. Tazewell is the Sidney, and Gen. Taylor the Herbert of the piece.

four, he was chosen, in May of the preceding year, the clerk of the Norfolk Courts. His skill in his business, the industry and integrity that shone in all his paths, his cordial and polished manners, his martial spirit, which approached something too near "an appetite for danger," but which was finely tempered to the social sphere, conciliated the public esteem; and, while he acquired the reputation of the readiest and the ablest clerk of his day, he became, during the excited period from 1802 to 1815, when war with Spain, with France, with England, was the order and the trouble of the day, one of the most complete soldiers of our citizen corps. Leaning to the federal side in politics, he, like the gallant Taylor, knew no party when the sword was to be drawn. At the early age of twenty-five he was made Colonel of the Ninth Regiment, was in active service during the Douglas war, as the affair that grew out of the affair with the Chesapeake was called, and, during the late war with Great Britain, commanded in the field the Second and Ninth Regiments, establishing an exactness of discipline and an *esprit du corps* which was a favorite topic of remark in the army. He was the soul of honor. His name was an authority, his word was a witness, wherever the one was known or the other uttered; and there were those who predicted for him, whether he should engage in the field or at the bar, a brilliant fame. Between him and Tazewell, who were nearly of the same age, the most affectionate friendship existed—a friendship which, founded on mutual esteem, and cemented by mutual kindness, has descended already to the third generation. In 1823, at the age of forty-seven, this excellent man passed away. I only knew him in his latter years and in my boyish days. I see him as, when our waters were filled with hostile fleets, he marched at the head of his regiment, on a horse richly caparisoned, shining with silver and steel. I see him as he walked along the street, a tall slim man, quick in his movements, and inspiring, by his air and gait and benignant eye, respect and even affection. He was early bald on the upper part of his head; but, by way of atonement, wore to the last, sometime after it was dropped by others, a long queue, that attracted the passing glance of the boys. He was, I think, except Seth Foster and Moses Myers, the last of the queues. He came of an old Anglo-Saxon stock. His name for centuries in Scotland

and in England had been borne by archbishops and illustrious laymen ; and in our own times, in the earlier part of this century, it was the synonym of British philanthropy. But neither early nor late, in the Old World or in the New, was it ever borne by a nobler or a purer man—a man over whose grave more gentle and more precious memories should hover—than WILLIAM SHARP.

When, in 1802, Tazewell appeared at the Norfolk bar, party politics were in a state of active fermentation. The passions of men became involved in the contests of the day to an extent which has not been reached since, and entered into the private relations of life. Men of business who had important cases for trial, and who were, for the most part, attached to the federal party, called in the aid of the federal members of the bar ; but it was soon seen that the young republican lawyer, who had voted for the resolutions of '98–'99, and for the report of '99–1800, and who had helped by his vote in the House of Representatives to elect Mr. Jefferson president, had introduced a new practice into the courts, and began to win verdicts in the greatest cases from all his federal opponents. The result was, as it always will be, that ability and learning prevailed over prejudice, and Tazewell was soon employed on the one or the other side of every great question. As an illustration of the strength of the political prejudices which prevailed, and which entered into domestic affairs, when Tazewell became a member of the Norfolk bar, I may mention an incident I heard many years ago. When it was rumored that Tazewell was paying his addresses to the eldest daughter of Col. Nivison, who belonged to the federal party, an old and active federalist observed that the Colonel would never allow a daughter of his to marry a democrat; and, as an illustration of the bigotry of the opposite party, I may mention that I have heard old republicans say that Tazewell's democracy was tainted by marrying into a federal family ; and that his marriage was the true explanation of the change of his relations with the administration of Jefferson, of which I shall treat in another place. And here it may be proper to state that, in 1802, Mr. Tazewell led to the altar Anne Stratton, the eldest daughter of Colonel John Nivison ; a lady with whom he lived most happily for fifty-four years, and whom, after an interval of eighteen months, he followed to the grave.

In the fall of 1803, William Wirt, whose brilliant genius has reflected so much credit on his adopted Commonwealth, came to reside in Norfolk. Like all his legal compatriots, he had been an active politician, and had been clerk of the House of Delegates for three sessions, during the last of which, the session of 1799, the Virginia report was adopted, and was a warm personal and political friend of Mr. Jefferson. It is from his pen that the beautiful resolutions of the Virginia Assembly, approving the administration of Jefferson at its close, proceeded ; but then he was not known even as the author of the Letters of the British Spy which, though they had been printed in the Richmond *Argus* in the early fall, had not been collected into a volume. He was welcomed most cordially by Mr. Tazewell, by whose persuasion he had come to Norfolk, and whose business was now so overflowing that he offered, as we are told by Wirt, to withdraw from several courts purely for his benefit. The success of Wirt was flattering, but, overcome by the fear of the yellow fever, and seduced by family attachments, in the early summer of 1806, he removed to Richmond. While he resided in Norfolk, he was engaged with Mr. Tazewell in the case of Shannon (1804), which was tried in Williamsburg, and which excited the most intense interest in Eastern Virginia. Of Mr. Tazewell's speech on the trial Mr. Wirt always spoke in terms of enthusiastic admiration, which was not the less glowing as until that time he had looked upon Mr. Tazewell only as a severe logician, and incapable of the loftier flights of eloquence. The buoyancy of Wirt's spirits is exhibited in his admirable letters published in the memoir of Mr. Kennedy ; and his gentle courtesy and generous nature are yet freshly remembered in our city. As a proof of his playfulness, I have heard Mrs. Tazewell say that when Wirt would call at her house, on his way to court, he would beg her for a bundle of newspapers to stuff in his green bag, to make a show of business as he passed into the court-house. When the Old Bachelor appeared, a series of essays in imitation of the Spectator, which Wirt published after leaving Norfolk, he delineated at full length the character of Tazewell, under the name of Sidney, and of General Taylor under that of Herbert ; and I refer to the number as a gratifying evidence of the estimate which he placed upon the genius and acquirements of those eminent men. And now that the grave has closed above Wirt and Tazewell, it is refreshing to contemplate the cordiality of their friendship, and the substantial welcome which Tazewell extended to Wirt; and it is proper to say that, but for the revelations of Mr. Wirt himself contained in his published letters, and in the statements of his nearest friends, the recollection of the generous kindness of Mr. Tazewell to Wirt, as may be said of many other cases, would have remained unknown to his surviving friends.

In tracing the career of a great lawyer, we should follow him through the courts in which his life was spent; but here, unfortunately, no records appear which can throw any light upon the subject. The grandest efforts of counsel are made in the presence of the court and of the jury, and of those spectators who may happen to be in the court-room at the time, and are soon forgotten. Many heroes, the poet tells us, lived before Agamemnon, but are forgotten, because they had no poet to record their praise; and, before the days of the stenographer, the most brilliant harangues in our inferior courts perished with the breath of them who uttered, and of those who heard them. Such has been the fate of Mr. Tazewell. Of all the speeches which he addressed to the courts and juries of Norfolk, from 1802 to 1821, not a vestige remains; and all that we know is, that he was employed on one side or other of all the important cases of that interval; and that he exhibited abilities which easily placed him at the head of the bar of the Commonwealth, and attracted the attention of all who, whether in foreign countries or our own, held any connexion with our city. I shall pass over his criminal cases altogether, though they abound in striking passages; and of his civil cases in the courts of the State during his practice, I shall select two only, and rather by way of allusion than in full detail, one of which was tried at the beginning of this period, and the other in 1821 near its close.

About the year 1798, an eccentric individual named John Taylor, but better known as Solomon John, to distinguish him from two other persons of the same name living in Norfolk at the same time, a man of wealth and position, but believed to be slightly deranged in some respects, was returning from a hunting excursion, and, stopping at Burk's Gardens, which have long since given way to the houses now composing Hartshorne's Court, deliberately discharged his piece, which was loaded with small shot, at a crowd of people, and wounded a man named Rainbow in the leg, which was at length amputated. Rainbow instituted a suit, an action of trespass on the case, in the Borough Court, and filed a declaration in that form. Tazewell, as Taylor's attorney, offered to demur to the declaration, a mode of pleading which, though old as the English law itself, was a novelty in the borough; and the Court refused to receive it. Mr. Tazewell took a bill of exceptions to the District Court at Suffolk. The point of the demurrer was that the action should have been trespass *vi et armis*. The District Court affirmed the decision of the Borough Court; and an appeal was taken to the Court of Appeals, which reversed the decision of the inferior courts. Until this time the distinction, which is merely technical, had been hardly perceptible to the courts of England and of this country, and was by no means settled law; but thereafter the points of difference were regarded as clearly defined; and both in England and in the courts of the United States, the case of Taylor vs. Rainbow has always been cited as conclusive of the question.

The other case, which was one of the last in which he appeared at the Virginia bar, was Long vs. Colston, and was argued in 1820, in the Court of Appeals. His associate in the case was Mr. Wickham, and the opposing counsel were Gen. Walter Jones and Mr. Stanard; and it was decided by Judges Roane, Cabell, and Coalter. The arguments of Tazewell are not stated; but Mr. Gilmer, who reports the decision, laments that no official reporter was present "to give to the profession even a sketch of the profound and comprehensive views of the counsel." The question was on the doctrine of Covenant; and I am told by learned counsel who have examined Mr. Tazewell's notes in the case, that this was, in their opinion, the greatest forensic display ever made in this country.

I recall an anecdote which was current at the time, and which shows the effect of Tazewell's argument on the court. Roane, one of the judges whose reputation has been held almost sacred in Virginia, was not prejudiced in favor of Tazewell, in consequence of old political feuds; but he was so transported by his argument that he could hardly think or speak of anything else during the day. It is said that, on the day of the argument, Roane had invited a party to dine with him, and after the adjournment of the court went to his study at home, where he appeared moody and abstracted. Meantime his company had arrived, and, as the Judge still lingered in his office, his wife went to him and informed him that the company was waiting; but all she could get from him were such broken sentences as these: "Yes, the first man that ever argued a law case," "the greatest of all our lawyers," "beyond all comparison our first lawyer;" while she, abandoning him to his reveries, led the guests to the table.

An incident which shows the character of Tazewell in an amiable point of view deserves a passing allusion. When he had retired for some time from general practice in our courts, he was induced to argue in the Superior Court in Portsmouth a memorable case of insurance in which he had been consulted; and, for the benefit of the junior members of the bar, he discussed all the difficult and leading points of the case at full length, and with all his ability, and made an impression upon the court, and upon the bar, which was gratefully and delightfully remembered.

The Cochineal case, rather from the rumors growing out of it, than from the case itself, which, however, embodied some important doctrines of the law of prize, and a large sum of money, deserves a passing allusion. The name of the case is the Santissima Trinidad, and the St. Andre, which was argued in the Supreme Court of the United States in 1822, on an appeal from the Circuit Court of Virginia, and is reported in seventh Wheaton (283–355). This was a libel filed by the Consul of Spain in the District Court of Virginia, in April, 1817, against 89 bales of cochineal, two bales of jalap, and one box of Vanilla, originally constituting part of the cargoes of the Spanish ships Santissima Trinidad and St. Andre, and alleged to be unlawfully and piratically taken out of those vessels on the high seas by a squadron consisting of two armed vessels, the Independencia del Sud, and the Altravida, under the command of Don Diego Chator, who sailed under a commission from the Government of the United Provinces of the Rio de la Plata—that Government having been, or being a dependency of Spain, and its independence not having been acknowledged by Spain or by the United States. Tazewell was employed by the Spanish Consul, M. Chacon, whose person is so familiar to our older citizens; and he gained the case in the Federal District and Circuit Courts, following it, contrary to his usual custom, to the Supreme Court. The case was argued in 1822, Winder and Ogden for the appellants, and Tazewell and Webster for the appellees. The questions involved were points of the law of prize, and are too technical for this presence ; but the speech of Tazewell, condensed and mutilated as it is in the report, is an admirable specimen of argument on purely legal topics which were to be worked out in the new political relations of the world, and to be settled by the law of nations. He gained the case in all the courts. John Randolph attended the trial in Washington, and was evidently alarmed at the trepidation which was always visible in Tazewell's manner on arising to address a court in a great case, and especially in a new scene, and felt some misgivings about the result. The trepidation, however, soon passed away ; and when Tazewell proceeded to establish point after point, and was in the full headway of his argument—a large audience, consisting of the ablest lawyers and statesmen of the Union, watching every syllable that fell from his lips, and following him through the mazes of his mighty plea—Randolph could restrain himself no longer, but said in a tone audible to those about him : "*I told you so—I told you so ; Old Virginny never tires.*"

It is known that Mr. Pinkney was engaged for the appellants ; and much interest was excited at the approaching contest between two men whose peculiar province was the law of admiralty ; but before the appointed time, Pinkney was summoned to another and higher tribunal ; and among those who deplored the loss which our whole country suffered in his death, none was more sincere than Mr. Tazewell. A friend, who had heard the current rumors concerning the death of Pinkney in connexion with the case, ventured to ask Mr. Tazewell about the truth of the matter. He instantly said that it was all a fiction,—that Pinkney, who was of a full temperament, died of an inflammatory disease (as we all know from his life by Wheaton); that there were no extremely difficult points in the case, and that, if there had been, Pinkney feared the face of no man living. Of Mr. Tazewell, intellectually and physically as he appeared at this time, an eloquent likeness is presented in the sketch of Francis Walker Gilmer.*

* See Appendix No. 3.

Tazewell had argued the Cochineal case in Norfolk and in Richmond before it reached the Supreme Conrt, and had exhibited such an abounding wealth of argument, it was believed that his last speech would be a mere reflection of its predecessors in the cause; but he was as wary as he was able; and, knowing from the magnitude of the case it would be carried up, and would be maintained by the greatest legal talents of the age, he wisely reserved some of his strongest points for the court of the last resort. When General Taylor, who went up to hear the final argument, returned to Norfolk, he told the bar, that to his surprise Tazewell had taken six new points in the case.

When M. Chacon, the Spanish Consul, called on Mr. Tazewell to engage him in behalf of the Spanish claimants, he was informed that he would undertake it in all the other points, if those connected with the then recent treaty with Spain, under which he had been appointed a commissioner by Monroe, were assigned to other counsel; and he suggested the name of Webster. He ever held the abilities of Mr. Webster in the highest respect; and when asked, on reaching Norfolk after the argument, what he thought of Webster, who was then, comparatively, a young man, he said he was excessively clever, but a lazy dog.

We now approach an epoch in the history of parties which materially involves the consistency of Mr. Tazewell as a politician. Although he had not been in public life since his withdrawal from Congress, he held no unimportant place in popular estimation. His course in the House of Delegates during four troublous years, and in the House of Representatives where he had taken an active and fearless part in the fierce strife for the election of a President, had commended him to the affections of that majority which has ruled the politics of Virginia since the adoption of the present federal constitution. He was the son of a beloved statesman who had fallen while in the innermost councils of that great party, and whose name was held in honor. His talents had now gained him a position among the ablest members of the bar; and his old political associates looked to him for aid in the crisis which was drawing near; and they looked in vain. This aspect of his political life it is my office to present before you.

Up to 1805 the administration of Jefferson was floating, to use one of his own figures, on the full tide of successful experiment. The obnoxious measures cf the federal party, where repeal was possible, had been repealed. The alien act, which Tazewell condemned not only as unconstitutional but to the last degree unwise, as tending to repress the emigration of those who would not only settle our waste lands, but to serve to defend the country during the crisis which he saw was rapidly approaching, and the sedition act, had expired by their own limitation. The judiciary act, which had been passed and carried into effect in the descending twilight of the late administration, had been repealed. Economy had been introduced into the public expenditures; and a considerable portion of the public debt had been extinguished. The foreign policy of the administration had been as successful as the domestic. Partly by chance, partly by that wise foresight which anticipates the possibilities of the future and provides for them, the administration had acquired from France the vast domain of Louisiana; and thenceforth the exclusive navigation of that mighty river, on which hitherto we dared not lift a sail or dip an oar without the consent of a foreign power, and on the banks of which, since its transfer from Spain to France, we had been vainly begging a place of deposit, became the birthright of every American citizen.

But this flattering prospect was soon to be overcast. England and France had long been at war; and, at the period of which we are treating, France had become the ruthless bandit of the land, and England the wanton pirate of the sea. Each desired the co-operation of the United States in the war—and each determined, in the event of our refusal to take part in the controversy in its favor, to cripple our commerce by all means within its reach. That commerce, fostered by our accidental position as neutrals when the two great commercial nations of the world were at war, had reached a marvellous height. Its keels vexed every sea. Its flag was now seen in the frozen circles; and now it reflected from its waving folds the fervors of the southern cross. Our merchants, springing, as it were, in a single night from the station of ordinary dealers and dependents on foreign countries to that of arbiters and rulers of the commerce of the globe, were equal to their new position; and our sailors, responsive to their will, gathered with their Briarean arms the wealth of every realm. Foreign statesmen in the recesses of the cabinet, and economists in the closet, beheld with amazement the rapid growth of our marine. They saw a nation, which had not then attained its seventeenth year, enjoying a commerce which nearly equalled in tonnage that which England had been gradually forming from the date of the Norman Conquest to that hour—a period of near eight hundred years. At such an epoch a strict neutrality in respect of the contending powers was the dictate alike of duty and interest. But such a policy was distasteful to England and France; and the result was the issuing of his successive decrees by Napoleon from Berlin and Milan, and the promulgation of the successive British orders in council. These iniquitous measures, the last mentioned of which, the British orders in council, have been since pronounced illegal by the courts of England herself, declared our ships with their cargoes forfeitable to England if they touched a French port, and to France if they touched a port in England or her dependencies.

In such a conjuncture opinions might well differ in respect of the proper means of redress. The administration of Jefferson sought it by long, able, and most urgent appeals to the sense of justice of the contending parties, but sought in vain. When mere diplomacy, though managed by the consummate ability and adroitness of William Pinkney at the court of St. James, and by our ablest men at the court of Napoleon, proved fruitless, the administration, at the earnest solicitation of its representatives at the hostile courts, determined to sustain our diplomatic action by such legislative measures as were likely to reach the interests of the contending powers. Non-intercourse and the embargo, which kept our ships in port, followed; and the administration, still pressing upon the belligerents the injustice and impolicy of their conduct, awaited the effect of their restrictive policy. Meantime its opponents were neither idle nor silent; and one long, universal cry rose from all the commercial cities. Their ships, the merchants said, were rotting at the wharf; if kept at home, they would soon become worthless; if sent to sea, they could but be taken. It was urged by the merchants that, even if England and France sequestered a number of their ships, still the profits earned by such as might escape confiscation would cover their losses on their investments. An able minority in Congress sustained the views held by the mercantile interest; but a large majority of both Houses of Congress, and of the people, approved the policy of the administration.

At this eventful moment a new political party, consisting almost wholly of Southern men, sprung into being. What added to its importance was, that, though ridiculously small in respect of the numbers who composed it, the members possessed great parliamentary eloquence and tact, and had previously been regarded as among the firmest friends of the administration. Its numbers were indeed so small both in Congress and out of it, as to exercise no weight in the call of the ayes and noes, or at the polls; but its members mingled in every debate, wrote plausible essays in the papers, and used all justifiable means as well as some that were questionable, in attaining their ends. Of this party, Mr. Tazewell, though never a member, and only a casual coadjutor, was considered to belong; but there was no evidence to show that he approved the vile scheme of its leaders of embroiling the country in a war with Spain. On the contrary, he held that the true remedy of existing grievances in the first instance was an immediate declaration of war against both belligerents, which, now that the curtain is lifted, we see was the true remedy of the hour; but that, if from prudence a declaration of war was withheld, it was unwise, by a total cessation of our most gainful commerce, to inflict upon our own people all the injuries which war would produce without any of the advantages that might accrue from a successful prosecution of hostilities; that the commercial regulations of England and France, though bearing disastrously on us, were chiefly designed to injure each other during actual war; and that, being war measures, they would determine on a restoration of peace, when we could obtain from the respective powers full redress for all our grievances.

He accordingly opposed the election of Mr. Madison to the presidency, whom he regarded as the impersonation of the restrictive policy which he had defended in his diplomatic writings, and from the press; and which was deemed the pledge of its continuance; and, in the spring of 1809, voted for the federal candidate for Congress, in opposition to Newton, who, though coming from a sea-port, had gallantly upheld the commercial policy of Jefferson, and who was returned by a decisive majority.

That epoch was the most mortifying in the annals of our country; and posterity must decide whether any action of ours could have averted the difficulty, and on whose shoulders the responsibility shall rest. When I reflect upon the incidents of that day; when I recount the millions of American capital sacrificed by the remorseless rapacity of England and France; when I call up from their graves the hundreds and thousands of American sailors, the sons of the men who had fought at Bunker Hill, who had led the forlorn hope at Stony Point, who had bled on the sweltering field of Eutaw, and who had stormed the outworks at York; when I reflect that such men were forcibly taken from their ships, and were compelled to fight the battles of England, to be doomed to the prison-ship, or to be scourged by the lash, and that not one dollar of those pilfered millions has yet been paid by one of the belligerents; and that all those injuries are yet unavenged;—passions, which I fondly hoped had long been quenched in my bosom, flame once more; and I am led to cherish with still deeper affection that Federal Union which will enable us henceforth to right such wrongs even though attempted by the combined navies of the world.

The same reasons which induced Mr. Tazewell to oppose the restrictive policy of the administrations of Jefferson and Madison, led him necessarily to oppose the war of 1812 with Great Britain. He believed that, if a declaration of war had been expedient at any period of the commercial difficulties with England and France, the proper time for declaring it was when the offence was given, and when our commerce was at the height, and our ability to sustain hostilities was proportionally greater; that the administration, having waived the opportunity of making a declaration in the first instance, and deliberately adopted the policy of diplomacy and of commercial regulation as the proper means of relief, our resources meantime having become crippled and our revenue almost annihilated, it was bound to adhere to it during the existing crisis; that the long and expensive war had impaired the resources of England and France, who would soon be compelled from mere exhaustion to make peace, and with the restoration of peace our difficulties would necessarily terminate, and we might demand redress for the grievances which we had sustained at their hands; that a declaration of war with England would be substantially, as it turned out to be, a receipt in full for our enormous commercial losses caused by her orders in council, which losses must then be assumed by our own government, or fall on the merchants, who would be crushed by their weight; that peace among the belligerents might happen at any moment, while a war with one of them would certainly involve a large expenditure of blood and money, and might continue at the pleasure of the belligerent long after a general pacification in Europe; and that, if war was to be waged as a measure of redress for our violated rights, as both belligerents were equally guilty, it should be declared against both.

In weighing the reasons on which any measure of public policy is founded, we must always refer to the time when the deed was done and to the position of the actors. At the present day, looking at the results which are believed to have flowed from the war of 1812, and especially our victories on the sea, we are inclined to blame those who opposed its declaration, and extol the wisdom and gallantry of those who approved it. This test, however, is neither philosophical nor just; and, as a proof of the soundness of Mr. Tazewell's opinions, or that at least they were not taken up, as has been alleged, from hostility to a democratic administration, we may state the fact that Madison himself, of whose administration the war shines as the crowning honor, was, like his predecessor in the presidency, opposed originally to its declaration; but was overruled or over-persuaded by the able and gallant young men whose eloquence carried that measure through Congress; and it should ever be remembered that, if the declaration had been postponed a few weeks, the repeal of the British orders in council would have rendered it unnecessary; and the thousands of precious lives and the millions of treasure which it cost would have been saved to the country.

If war, with all its possible compensations, be at all times a dangerous and uncertain measure—if all the treasures and glories which human hands can hold, and the imaginations of men may compute, in the estimation of the true patriot as well as the true

Christian, sink into dust, when compared with the unnecessary and wanton sacrifice of the life of the humblest citizen of the Republic—if the war with England cost millions of wealth, and the shedding of the blood of tens of thousands of our fellow-men,—then it is something to say that, if the policy of Tazewell had been pursued for a few weeks—a policy which, so far as war was concerned, had been, up to its declaration, the deliberate policy of Jefferson and Madison—that war which had been postponed to the dawn of the pacification in Europe, would not have occurred.

The question for posterity to decide is, not whether, if we judge by results, Tazewell was right or wrong—a mode of judging too fallacious and too dangerous in human affairs, and subjecting the responsibility of human actors to too fearful a test,—but which, even if applied to the course of Mr. Tazewell, would confirm, beyond question, the wisdom of the policy which he advised at the time; but the question is, whether his policy was not such as a great statesman, intent solely upon the welfare of his country, might not have pursued, not only without impairing the public confidence in his patriotism, integrity, and attachment to the cardinal principles of his political faith, but such as, even with the facts then before him, reflected high credit upon his sagacity and courage.

But whatever were his views about the policy of declaring war at any particular time, no sooner was war declared than he gave it a cordial support. In concert with the administration, and in connection with his friend and associate, Gen. Taylor, to whom was assigned the command of the forces at Norfolk, he exerted all his powers to put our port in a posture of defence. He hailed, especially, our victories on the sea with enthusiastic applause, and ever rejoiced that the treaty of Ghent was preceded, at least in this country, by the glorious Eighth of January.

To confirm the remark that Mr. Tazewell, though opposed to the restrictive policy of Jefferson, was still friendly to that statesman, and was unwilling to be considered hostile to him, I may recall to the recollection of my elder hearers an incident which created much amusement when it occurred. It appears that, in the winter of 1807, when Tazewell had been sent to the Assembly to attend to some local interests of Norfolk, a caucus of the republican members had been called in Richmond with a view of denouncing those who opposed the restrictive policy as deserters from the party. When the night of the caucus arrived, Tazewell, who was confined to his bed by sickness, heard of the gathering for the first time. Ill as he was, he hastened to the place of meeting, and, with his head bound with napkins, and in haggard attire, made his appearance in the middle of the caucus. The clever young men who then managed the machinery of the party were struck dumb by his presence as by that of an apparition. Then Tazewell spoke. He reasoned upon the impolicy of forcing a third party into existence, when, while he was speaking, the winds might bear over the waters the revocation of the British orders and the French decrees, and all would be well. He showed that, while he disapproved a single measure of the administration, he heartily approved its general policy, and the constitutional doctrines which composed its faith. There was no reply. The meeting dispersed, and my democratic friends have ever since been cautious how they undertook to read clever fellows out of the party.

In 1807 occurred one of those painful incidents which roused the people of that day to madness—which fills the heart, even at this late day, with pain and sadness, but which has such a connection with Mr. Tazewell, that I, a Norfolk man, addressing Norfolk men, cannot pass it by in silence. On the early morn of the 22d of June, a frigate, built by your own mechanics, in sight of your city, baptized in the waters of your own Elizabeth, bearing the name of your own noble bay, and under the command of as gallant a Virginian as ever trod a deck, lifting her anchor in the Roads, put out to sea on the errand of her country. On the following day, unsuspecting of danger, she was attacked by the British frigate Leopard, and became her prize. The commander of the Leopard, when he had taken from the Chesapeake certain men whom he alleged were deserters from the British flag, declined to take further possession of the captured frigate, which returned to the Roads. Three of our men were killed, and sixteen wounded, during the attack. These wounded men were brought to the marine hospital, and received every possible attention. One of them died, and was buried with all the solemnities of public sorrow.

When the fatal tidings were known, there arose a piercing shriek of agony and grief, followed presently by the low, touching wail from the stricken heart of the nation. And then, the louder and the longer for the delay, came the cry for vengeance, which burst from the lips of a whole people. The promptness and dispatch with which the British frigate acted indicated deliberate design; and the suspicion instantly flashed across the public mind that the consular authorities of England in our port were privy to its execution. The outbreak in Norfolk was terrible. Had Col. Hamilton, the consul, not been long and intimately known and loved by the people, he would have been taken from his house and gibbeted on the square, as an expiation of the blood of our countrymen, wantonly shed, in a time of peace, by a British captain. An unfortunate British officer, who came up from one of the four frigates in the bay, had well-nigh been torn in pieces by the infuriated people. In such a conjuncture the ordinary forms of government were overlooked, and the citizens in full assembly, the venerable Mathews in the chair, appointed, as in the days of the Revolution, a Committee of Safety. A preamble, setting forth in becoming terms the outrage on the Chesapeake, was adopted, and it was resolved that there should be no intercourse with the British frigates in our waters, or with their agents, until the decision of the federal government was known, under the penalty of being deemed infamous; and the Committee of Safety, consisting of fourteen of our most worthy citizens, some of whose descendants are now within the sound of my voice, were authorized to take such measures as the emergency demanded.*

As soon as Commodore Douglas read the resolves of the Norfolk meeting, he addressed an insolent note to the mayor of the borough, in which he declared that if the resolutions were not *instantly annulled*, he would prohibit every vessel bound in or out of Norfolk from proceeding to her place of destination. This letter was written on board the Bellona frigate, on the third of July. "You are aware," said this haughty Briton, "that the British flag

* The committee were Thomas Mathews, Thomas Newton, Jr., Luke Wheeler, Theodoric Armistead, Richard E. Lee, Moses Myers, William Pennock, William Newsum, Thomas Blanchard, Daniel Bedinger, Seth Foster, J. W. Murdaugh, Richard Blow, and Francis S. Taylor.

never has, nor ever will be insulted with impunity." After some further remarks, he adds: "It therefore rests with the inhabitants of Norfolk either to engage in a war, or remain on terms of peace.' And he closed his letter by saying that he had proceeded with his squadron, which consisted of four fifty-gun frigates, to Hampton Roads, to await the answer of the mayor of Norfolk, which he hoped would be forwarded without delay.

It is in this stage of the proceedings, which he probably regulated from the first, that I shall introduce Mr. Tazewell to your notice. No community was ever placed in a more delicate dilemma. The stoppage of our commerce would produce great inconvenience, and there was no force which the federal government could command at all competent to raise the embargo; and at any moment blood might be shed. The people, meantime, were in a tempest of rage. I have heard, from men who saw those times, that, if the British commodore had put his threat in execution—if, in so doing, as would have been inevitable, he had taken another human life, or shed another drop of American blood, not only would war have followed, but something worse than war, which, even at this distance of time, we tremble to contemplate. The blood of innocent Englishmen would have been shed everywhere as a propitiation to the manes of our murdered countrymen. Under these circumstances Tazewell dictated the celebrated letter of the mayor of Norfolk, which was admired over the whole country, not only for its spirit, but for the admirable tact with which it put the British commodore in the wrong. That letter, which was written on the Fourth of July, begins with this paragraph:

"Sir, I have received your menacing letter of yesterday. The day on which this answer is written ought of itself to prove to the subjects of your sovereign that the American people are not to be intimidated by menace; or induced to adopt any measures except by a sense of their perfect propriety. Seduced by the false show of security, they may be sometimes surprised and slaughtered, while unprepared to resist a supposed friend. That delusive security is now passed forever. The late occurrence has taught us to confide our safety no longer to anything than to our own force. We do not seek hostility, nor shall we avoid it. We are prepared for the worst you may attempt, and will do whatever shall be judged proper to repel force, whensoever your efforts shall render any act of ours necessary. Thus much for the threats in your letter."

Of this letter Tazewell was appointed to be the bearer, and, attended by a friend whose son is now a leading member of our bar,* delivered it to Commodore Douglas on board the Bellona frigate in the presence of the captains of the fleet. An account of the scene is fortunately preserved by his own pen in a letter to the Mayor; and it is plain to see that the British captains, among whom was Sir Thomas Hardy, to whom Lord Nelson addressed in his dying moments that affectionate request, surprised and overwhelmed by the address and ability of Tazewell, recanted all their threats; and in their letter of the 5th breathed nothing but amity and peace. Whoever will read the letter of Commodore Douglas of the 3d of July, and his letter of the 5th, will see the most amusing instance of backing out in the annals of diplomacy. The federal government now took the case in hand, and the committee of safety in an eloquent address resigned the authority with which they had been invested by the people.

One of the obvious results of the peace of 1815 with Great Britain was the active employment of our commercial marine. During the war the seeds of new enterprises had been sown, and much of that capital which had previously been employed in navigation had been diverted, and fresh capital was required in its place. There was a general desire for the creation of new banks; and as the principles of banking, which have become more familiar since, were in 1816 comparatively unknown to those who composed a majority of the assembly, it was important that Norfolk should be ably represented in the assembly. At this time the existing banks, which had suspended during the war, had not resumed the payment of specie. On the subject of banks, Tazewell, though brought up by men who had been almost ruined by a paper currency and hated the name, his own father having been one of the most active statesmen in forcing a resumption of specie payments after the peace of 1783, was not unwilling that commercial

* Tazewell Taylor, Esq.

men should employ the agency of banks under proper restrictions; and having been elected by the people of Norfolk to the House of Delegates without his knowledge and during his absence from home, he took his seat in that body in 1816. Let it be remembered, that when he took this trust from the people of Norfolk, he was constantly engaged in the highest duties of his profession; that he was not only employed in courts, but was consulted by foreign clients—by the merchants of London and by the Court of Rome; and that his absence from town in the performance of his duties in the assembly would result in the loss of thousands at a time when he was far from being a wealthy man; and we will have some idea of the principles which guided his conduct in respect of the public service. He sought nothing—he asked nothing from public bodies or from the people, but he recognized the obligation resting on every citizen to serve his country; and when an emergent case occurred, and he was called out by the people, he never declined office, but entered into it at every personal sacrifice, performing its duties with such success and such ability as to leave an impression upon the times in which he lived.* He practically defeated the wild banking schemes of the session by the insertion of a specie clause which was readily adopted by the friends of those measures, but which, as was designed, made their schemes impracticable.

But his great effort in the assembly of 1816 was his speech on the Convention bill of that year. He spoke in reply to the late Gen. Smythe of Wythe; and in an argument of uncommon power, which formed one of the eloquent traditions of the House when I took my seat in it twelve years later, he answered the objections urged against the existing constitution, and sustained that instrument in all its length and breadth. His speech produced a wonderful effect upon all who heard it. The late Philip Doddridge, one of the ablest and most decided of all Mr. Tazewell's opponents in state and federal politics, but ever abounding in that magnanimity which flourishes most in the finest minds, always spoke of the argument of Mr. Tazewell in reply to Gen. Smythe as extraordinary—as surpassing any that he ever heard in a deliberative

* For his views of public duty see Appendix No. 4.

assembly. He told me so in conversation, and he afterwards spoke of it in the same exalted strain in the House of Delegates and in the Convention of 1829. The result of the Convention discussion was, that, though a bill calling a Convention passed the House by a small majority, it was lost in the Senate ; and a compromise was effected between the East and the West by reorganizing the basis of representation in the Senate on white population according to the census of 1810. In this as on most other occasions the testimony magnifying the speeches of Tazewell come from a hostile quarter.

His election to the Senate of the United States in 1824 was one of the severest trials of his life. Having withdrawn alike from the inferior and appellate courts, he anxiously desired to spend the remainder of his days in the bosom of his family, and to mingle no more in public affairs. To undertake any special service in behalf of his country was always a grateful employment ; but to leave his home for months, and to be engaged in the monotonous routine of deliberative bodies, was most distasteful to him ; but, true to the great maxim of his life—never to seek or to decline a public trust—he accepted the appointment ; and took his seat in the early part of January, 1825. A casual view of his career in that body, which extended from 1825 to 1833—a period of nearly eight years—during which he held, at least in the estimation of Virginia, if not of the whole Union, the foremost place, would alone occupy the brief hour allotted me on the present occasion. The exciting questions of that exciting period would pass in review ; and the ashes are too thinly spread over the smouldered fires of those days yet to be trodden with safety, and certainly not with pleasure by some of those who hear me, and who heartily joined in decreeing a tribute to the memory of Mr. Tazewell. I will merely allude to two or three speeches and writings, which the student of history may consult as specimens of parliamentary ability, and as eminently displaying the caste of Mr. Tazewell's intellectual character as well as his views on political subjects.

His *début* in the Senate was made on the bankrupt bill of that session—not a regular speech, but a searching examination of the details of the bill, which he exposed with such effect that its friends substantially gave it up in despair. His first serious speech was delivered on the 21st day of the same month in which he had taken his seat, on his own motion to strike out the third section of the bill for the suppression of piracy in the West India seas, which had been reported from the Committee of Foreign Affairs, and had been introduced by a forcible speech from its chairman, who was also his colleague—a name to be pronounced with respect by every Virginian—the venerable James Barbour then the acknowledged head of the Senate. The section proposed to be stricken out authorized the President of the United States in a time of profound peace to declare, on the representations of a naval officer, any of the ports of Spain in the West Indies in a state of blockade. The bill was likely to pass without serious opposition, when it arrested the attention of Mr. Tazewell, who, then fresh from his great discussions of the law of prize, exposed the danger of its provisions in an argument which at once placed him at the head of the Senate, and was read, though in a mutilated report, by the whole country, with admiration and applause. The effect of the speech may be seen in the fact that the obnoxious section, though upheld by the eloquent and patriotic patron of the bill, by the gallant Hayne and by others, was stricken out by the decisive vote of 37 to 10. Had it remained in the bill, in less than ninety days it might have produced a war with Spain.*

* This speech Mr. Tazewell was surprised to learn from the public prints, was regarded as a great effort. In a letter dated the 3d of February, 1825, a few days after the delivery of the speech, he writes to a friend in Virginia as follows: "The newspapers and my Virginian friends have done me irreparable mischief in the too lavish encomia they have bestowed upon my speech, as you call it. Believe me, I was very much in the situation of him who had been talking prose all his life without knowing it. I had no conception that I had made a speech, and really thought I had merely given a clear and distinct exposition of a matter of public law as familiar to me as the doctrine of dower, and concerning which I had no more doubt. And it was with infinite astonishment I first saw the strong panegyric heaped upon my argument here. So true is this, that on the evening after I had concluded it, I wrote to my friend Wickham, telling him if his eye should see anything of it through the newspapers, he would wonder how so much A B C knowledge could be tolerated here, but that I saw it was necessary to state it, and therefore he must not think me so much of a pedant as he might otherwise be disposed to do. Had the thing been suffered to pass unnoticed, I might have hoped at some time or other to gain some credit for a speech when I saw an occasion offered to make one; and I have vanity enough to believe that I could make a much better almost any day of the week."

On the election of Mr. John Quincy Adams to the Presidency, and especially after the delivery of his first message to Congress, he became hostile to his administration, and opposed its prominent measures. His most remarkable performance was his speech on the exclusive constitutional competency of the executive to originate foreign missions without the advice and consent of the Senate. As a constitutional thesis, without respect to the time of delivery, —for, although Mr. Adams asserted the power, he at the same moment waived its exercise,—as a specimen of his manner of treating a great constitutional question when numerous authorities and precedents are to be examined and set aside, this speech deserves to be studied. With the exception of Gen. Marshall's speech in the case of Jonathan Robbins, it stands preëminent in our political literature as a model of profound research, of thorough argumentation, and of overwhelming strength. The reader at this day feels that he is borne along by a force which is not only equal to the occasion, but above it, and which it is vain to resist. The speech is no mean system of logic and of the rules of evidence in itself. And in connection with this speech I may mention the speech on the same subject, which he delivered some years later, in reply to Mr. Livingston, and in which the topic is discussed with new illustrations. These two speeches alone survive in any fulness of all his forensic exertions. The speech which Mr. Tazewell himself thought the best he ever delivered in the Senate, was on some one of the bankrupt bills of his term of service; but of this speech not a passage can now be found.

Nor would it be practicable to present here even a condensed view of the reports which he drew either as the head or as a member of the Committee of Foreign Affairs. Almost any one of those reports would have built up a respectable reputation for its author. I shall only specify his report on the Panama mission, which mainly settled the public mind in relation to that measure;

He complains of the bad Latin the papers put in his mouth, and of such expressions as "three twins," &c., &c. I grieve to think that so few specimens of Mr. Tazewell's arguments are to be found in print. I have heard from him year after year, in conversation, arguments on current or general topics, which, if emblazoned through the press, would make a fair reputation for a speaker, and he all unconscious at the time that he was making any considerable effort.

and his report on the Colonization Society, in which, incidentally—and by the way, he demonstrated conclusively the constitutional right of the United States to acquire territory. When it is remembered that Mr. Jefferson took a different view of this question at the time of the acquisition of Louisiana, and believed an amendment to the constitution necessary to the validity of the purchase; the originality as well as the ability of Mr. Tazewell appear in a favorable light.

Meantime his reputation had been extending far and wide. In Virginia some of our older politicians had not become, nor were they ever, fully reconciled to him in consequence of his course during the administrations of Jefferson and Madison; but these were gradually disappearing from the stage, and he now seemed to be regarded by the great body of the people as the most popular man of his time; and he was reëlected unanimously to the Senate, or, to speak with strictness, with only four scattering votes. One instance may show the height on which he stood at this time. His second election to the Senate was made the order of the day for the 1st of January, 1829: the day had come; the order was about to be read from the chair; and I was about to rise in my place in the House of Delegates to nominate him for reëlection, when a gentleman, advanced in life, who had rendered valuable service to his country, hailing, too, from a central part of the State, came to my seat and implored me to allow him, as the crowning honor of his life, to nominate Mr. Tazewell for reëlection. I think I may safely affirm, from close observation at the time both at home and abroad, that the abilities and character of Mr. Tazewell were held in higher estimation, and even veneration, in Virginia and out of it, at this period, than those of any of her statesmen since the retirement of Jefferson and Madison from the public service. It was a commingled feeling of admiration, awe, and pride.

It is a coincidence in the lives of Mr. Tazewell and his father, that the father was elected to the Senate of the United States to fill a vacancy caused by the resignation of John Taylor of Caroline; and that the son, after an interval of thirty years from the election of the father, was chosen to fill the vacancy in the Senate made by the resignation of the same individual; and that father and son were twice elected president of the Senate.

The views of Mr. Tazewell on the important topics which arose out of the efforts of South Carolina in relation to the tariff policy of the federal government, can only be alluded to in the briefest manner. He was opposed to the doctrine of nullification as expounded by the South Carolina school of politicians, and did not regard it as a peaceful and constitutional mode of redress; while he condemned the doctrines of the Proclamation of Gen. Jackson as destructive of the rights of the States, and as opposed to the true theory of our federal system. In a series of numbers which appeared in the Norfolk Herald and were republished in the Richmond Enquirer, he traced in the most elaborate of his compositions extant the history of the formation of the present federal constitution, and expounded its theory in a strain of argument as nearly approaching a demonstration as topics of that nature allow. These articles were published in pamphlet form at the time; and, with the exception of the numbers of Senex which appeared in the Herald and Enquirer, and were republished in pamphlet in England, and reviewed in the London Quarterly, on the policy of Mr. Adams' administration respecting the West India trade, are the only serial contributions, as far as I know, he ever made to the periodical press.

The only one of the vexed questions which harassed the administration of Gen. Jackson that Mr. Tazewell, after his retirement from the Senate, discussed in public, was the removal of the deposits from the Bank of the United States by the Treasury order of October, 1833. The reasons of the Secretary of the Treasury for issuing that order were communicated in detail to Congress on the 3d of December following; and his report was discussed in both Houses for several months with an ability and warmth never before displayed in a congressional discussion. The people caught the excitement; and public meetings were held in all the commercial cities; and memorials were forwarded to Congress urging the immediate restoration of the deposits to the vaults of the bank. Each memorial, as it was received by a Senator or Representative, was honored with a speech from some master spirit. And now the most menacing monetary crisis occurred which the country had ever seen. In a little less or more than six months the Bank of the United States had shortened its line of discounts ten millions of dollars; and all the State banks in self-defence were compelled to follow the example of that great institution. Confidence ceased to exist. No man in business could look ahead a single day without fear and trembling. Men spoke in whispers, and walked doubtfully as if the earth might quake beneath their feet. The result was a change in the party relations of those who lived in towns without a parallel in our history. And it was soon seen that a new party was forming in comparison of which the *tertium quid* party of Jefferson's administration was a mere bubble floating on the surface of the stream. In that tempest was rocked the cradle of that large and intellectual party, which assumed the appellation of Whig, which won some splendid victories, which encountered some decisive defeats, which then slept awhile, and which has recently burnished its armor anew for a fresh campaign.

Richmond set the example among us of holding meetings of the people, with a view of urging the restoration of the deposits to the Bank. Watkins Leigh and Chapman Johnson made on that occasion an appeal to the people of Virginia in favor of a restoration, which was heard from so respectable a source with the attention it deserved. The Assembly then in session, which, when elected, had been favorable to the administration of Jackson, faltered in their faith, instructed the senators in Congress to vote for a restoration of the deposits, and on the resignation of Mr. Rives, who upheld the policy of the administration, elected Mr. Leigh in his stead. Even the *Richmond Enquirer*, its polar star momentarily obscured, was tossing helplessly on that tempestuous sea.

In this state of things, some of the citizens of Norfolk, of both parties, as those parties had previously stood, highly distinguished by social position, by talents, by wealth, and by their intimate connection with our banking institutions, called on Mr. Tazewell, and requested him to take the chair at a public meeting to be held on the 8th of January, 1834. He consented to do so, and on taking the chair delivered one of the most graceful, most nervous, and most eloquent speeches that ever fell from his lips. In language not to be misunderstood, he denounced the act of removing the deposits from the Bank of the United States, advised their immediate restoration, and condemned the whole series of the measures of the President of the United States in relation thereto. A gentleman happening to be present who had heard Canning, Brougham, and Sir Robert Peel from the hustings and in the House of Commons, declared that the speech of Mr. Tazewell fully equalled their grandest efforts on such occasions; and all who heard it pronounced it a wonderful work of argument, eloquence, and declamation combined. A few days after the meeting, Mr. Tazewell was elected Governor of the Commonwealth.

The conduct of Mr. Tazewell on this occasion I leave to history. It was my misfortune to differ from him, and to strive against him in public meetings, by resolutions, by speeches, and by essays in the public prints, and to have been on the side of the victorious party; and I owe it to candor to say that, after a deliberate investigation of the arguments and the circumstances of that time with such faculties as God has bestowed upon me, my views through the twenty-seven years that have since passed remain unaltered; but now that my illustrious friend is gone, and as I measure that chasm which his death has made in the Commonwealth, leaving none equal to him or like him behind, and especially in my own bosom—a chasm which, at my time of life, can never, never be closed—I have looked with fear and trembling over all I said and wrote on that occasion, and I am gratified to find that, although I spoke with as great freedom of men and things as the occasion, in my opinion, demanded, I spoke personally of Mr. Tazewell as a son should speak of a father, and with that exalted respect with which I ever regarded his colossal character.

Still, if Mr. Tazewell had been a man of narrow mind, our friendship would have ended, and the instruction and delight which I have derived from his conversation for the last twenty-seven years—a period in which I have doubled my own age—would have been lost. But, independent himself, and the proudest man I ever knew when the faintest shadow of vassalage was sought to be cast upon him, he valued independence in others, and his wide experience taught him that the friend who would not hesitate to stand up firmly against him when he thought him wrong, would be the last to skulk from his side in the hour of danger, and from the defence of his memory when his head was low.

While I leave the wisdom of his course in relation to the deposit question and in the executive chair of the commonwealth to the award of history, I recall one lesson which may be read from his acts, which is, that he never was, strictly speaking, a party man; that while he held to his dying day the theory of our federal system which he had adopted in his youth, and in defence of which he prepared, as has just been said, in his old age, with his vast stores of learning and experience unrolled before him, the most elaborate and conclusive exposition which that system ever received; his course on the restrictive policy and on the removal of the deposits, irrespective as it was whether he carried along with him one or a thousand of his associates, shows that on great questions involving mere expediency he would burst the trammels of party, and act with his old and inveterate opponents against the darling measures of his political friends. I have said that he was not, and could not well be, in a series of years, the unvarying adjunct of any party. He looked upon a subject through so many lights,—the lights of the past, the lights of the present, the lights of the future; he saw such a tissue of good and evil so inextricably intermingled in human projects; he saw so much that was questionable in the best party measures; so much that was not bad in what seemed the worst; and so much that could be accomplished by doing nothing, that, though he was prompt above most men in decision, and to the last degree practical, his enthusiasm was cooled by philosophy, and he was never very much exalted or depressed by the success or failure of political schemes.

While Mr. Tazewell was engaged in his senatorial career, he was elected by the Norfolk district a member of the Convention which assembled in Richmond on the fifth day of October, 1829, to revise the first Constitution of Virginia. The character of that body is familiar to all; some of the most illustrious names recorded in our annals were inscribed upon its rolls,—Madison, Marshall, Monroe, Watkins Leigh, Charles Fenton Mercer, Chapman Johnson, Philip Doddridge, Robert Stanard, Philip P. Barbour, Morris, Fitzhugh, Baldwin, Scott, Cooke—that wonderful man whose train was always tracked by fire, John Randolph, and a host of younger statesmen who have since risen to eminence, and who, like their elder colleagues, have, I am grieved to think, nearly all passed away, were among the members, and were engaged day after day, for three months and a half, in performing the office which their country had committed to their hands. The most distinguished men of the Union,—statesmen whose own names were historical, men of letters, merchants who remembered that the wealth of the counting-room and the wealth of statesmanship were indissolubly bound together, old planters, clever young men from Virginia and from nearly all the southern States, came to behold its meeting, to see its members, and to hear the debates; and, as if to invest the scene with a yet lovelier hue, beauty, brightened by intelligence and glowing with patriotism, shed its softened light over that imposing spectacle. In that body, in which an ex-president of the United States presided, in which another ex-president was at the head of a committee, in which the chief justice of the United States was at the head of another committee, in which there was no place of honor for judges, governors, ministers to foreign courts, speakers of the House of Representatives, and senators of the United States, above their fellow-members, the eye of the visitor soon singled out Mr. Tazewell. He was the grandest figure of a man among them all. His fame was then at the height, and his large stature, his full stern features, lighted by a wide grave blue eye, his solemn gait, all inspiring awe as he leaned in his seat or passed through the hall—were in fair keeping with that intellectual image of him which had previously existed in the mind of the beholder.

To trace with any minuteness the course of Mr. Tazewell through more than three of the most anxious months of his life would far exceed my present limits, and as I have already treated this topic in a separate work, and have been required to treat it again, I shall simply say here, that Mr. Tazewell made the opening speech in support of a resolution which he offered, and which marked out the course of the campaign which he believed to be best adapted to attain the general end in view. Had that resolution been adopted, I now believe, as I believed then, that a constitution would have been formed which would have lasted for half a century, and that Tazewell, as a skilful and fearless medi-

5

ator between the East and West, would have performed the office with glorious success. But the passions of men raged high; extremes were the order of the day, and each party stood pledged to its favorite scheme. His first regular effort on the floor of the Convention was in reply to Mr. Monroe, and gave him the opportunity of expounding his theory of interests as the basis of a political system—a system as beautiful as true. His speech presented a fair specimen of what the discussions on the basis question ought to have been—not of the elaborate dissertation which lasted two days, but of the vigorous living speech, which, while it reviewed critically intermediate points in passing, kept the main subject steadily in view, and of which the House of Commons has afforded us so many illustrations. When the house rose, a gentleman, who was perhaps the most accomplished scholar in the State, said to me that the speech of Tazewell was the first truly parliamentary speech delivered during the session, and drew the distinction between a legitimate debate and a disoussion by dissertations. I recall a happy effort of Mr. Tazewell on the subject of the election of governor by the people, which was possessed of singular beauty and order. The effect of that speech was the settlement of the question.

But the occasion which impressed his hearers most deeply with a sense of his abilities, was a discussion on the tenure of the judicial office, in which Chief Justice Marshall, Philip P. Barbour, Stanard, Scott, Giles, and others took part. Each speaker was conscious of the powers of his opponent; posterity, in the presence of the skilful reporter, as well as the existing generation represented by some of the ablest men, were the spectators of the combat; and a visible air of solemnity pervaded the manner of each. The question was precisely that which sprung from the repeal of the judiciary act of 1800 by the Congress of 1802, and is the nicest of all our party questions. It was a magnificent display of parliamentary tact and intellectual vigor; and I do not think that an hour of my life ever glided so insensibly away as while I listened to that debate. Blows fell fast and heavy. I saw Judge Barbour, who, though president of the Convention, as the house was in committee, engaged in the debate, fairly reel in his seat from one of Judge Marshall's massy blows, which he returned presently with right good will; but Tazewell, if I may use a figure which presented the pith of the argument of one side, and which was frequently used by both,—Tazewell fairly "*sunk the boat*" under the Chief Justice. The views of Tazewell prevailed; and in such a contest, in which all were kingly, and in which the combatants were *magis pares quam similes*—rather equals than alike—if the victor's wreath could with propriety be awarded to a single individual, I do not think I err in saying that it would have been assigned by a majority of the hearers to Tazewell. As an illustration of the effect of his manner and argument on the minds of able men who were opposed to him in State politics, which then raged fiercely, a gentleman from the West, who held for several years a seat in the House of Delegates and in the Council, speaking of the debate to me on the day it occurred, said: "Why, Tazewell trod down those great men as if they had been children."

When the Convention adjourned *sine die*, every heart melted, and all animosity soothed by the last words of the president, I saw Tazewell approach Madison and Marshall, and exchange parting salutations. He could go no further; the members pressed round him: but, old as he then was, for he had reached his 56th year, he little dreamed that he was destined to outlive almost all of those young and gallant spirits that then loved and greeted him. He was the last survivor of those who sate in the House of Delegates during the eighteenth century; and of the Convention of 1829, out of 96 members who composed it, he attained to a greater age than has yet been attained by any member of the body, not excepting Madison, whom he exceeded by one month and five days, and surviving all but twenty; and three of that twenty have come here this day to honor his memory.*

Perhaps the best description of his manner at the bar would be to say that he had no manner at all. In addressing juries, he talked to them, I am told, ordinarily as he would converse with the same number of men in society on the merits of the case; and his gestures were those which might be used without serious remark in animated conversation. His postures were sometimes

* Ex-President Tyler, who was the third, was unexpectedly prevented from being present: the Hon. George Loyall and the speaker were the other two.

negligent enough; he had a contempt for rant, and hated show and pomp. His voice was pleasant, and of ample compass for an ordinary court-room, and he never dealt in vociferations; indeed, his style of argument to the jury, as well as to the bench, would have been impossible to a boisterous talker. While his manner was natural, his matter seemed equally void of art. When by the examination and cross-examination of witnesses, he had obtained his facts, he formed his theory of the case, and unfolded it to the jury in the simplest possible way. It was plain to see, however, that the argument was a continuous chain of demonstration, every link of which seemed to be of equal strength. Some of his speeches to the jury, could they have been preserved as they were delivered, would have been invaluable specimens of dialectics for the use of students. I heard the late William Maxwell say, that it was vain and even fatal to attempt before a jury to find the defective links in the chain of Mr. Tazewell's arguments, for the process would become too refined for their comprehension; and that his own mode of argument in such cases was to let the reasoning of Tazewell pass, and press with all his force some plain views of the case. Some lawyers are successful in the elenchical mode of argument—to use a logical term—that is, in demolishing the structure of their opponents, while they fail in the deictic, that is, in raising on its ruins an impregnable fabric of their own; but it was difficult to decide which process was the most thorough in the reasoning of Tazewell. In putting his arguments before a jury he showed great adroitness. He either knew himself or learned from others the calling of every juryman; and as he proceeded with his case, if he saw a dangerous man among them, he drew his figures from his particular calling, and not unfrequently made the man believe that his standing in his own business depended upon his bringing in a verdict in his favor. When the passions were to be assailed, he indulged in a style of fervid appeal which was the more effective as it was rare; and his speech in Shannon's case was often referred to by Wirt as a fine piece of eloquence in the popular acceptation of the word.

His mode of addressing the bench differed, of course, from his jury speeches. He was less familiar in his manner and in his talk, and his argumentation was more severe; and he was evidently more at home, or rather more congenially employed ; and he brought as much learning to bear upon the case as was politic for the time. Here, too, he showed no great deference to manner as a means of victory. When Gen. Taylor was addressing the late judge St. George Tucker, who was deaf, the judge requested him to come nearer and speak louder ; but the General, observing that a certain space between the judge and himself was indispensable for the proper exercise of his faculties, declined the request ; Tazewell, however, who replied to Taylor, had no scruples in the case, but, approaching the judge's ear, poured the stream of his argument into its inner portal. It sometimes appeared that in addressing inferior courts he went too much into detail, instead of resting his case on its great points ; but it is probable that Mr. Tazewell had taken the true gauge of the judge's mind, and was right after all ; and it is certain that in important cases, in which appeals would probably be taken, he reserved his strong points for the higher tribunal.

Those who heard even his latest speeches at the bar have almost all passed away. It was thirty-four years ago that I heard him for the first time in public. At a meeting of the citizens of Norfolk, held in the Town Hall, to give expression to their feelings on the occasion of the death of Jefferson, which occurred on the Fourth of July, 1826, he was called to the chair, and, before taking it, addressed the large assembly for twenty-five or thirty minutes, on the character of the great man whose death they had met to commemorate. He was at that time a senator of the United States, and in the height of his fame ; and to hear him speak was then a great novelty, which attracted hundreds to the hall. Though then a youth of nineteen, I can recall his manner and the outline of his speech. He seemed to speak as a man of fine personal appearance accustomed to public speaking and of a good address, who was deeply impressed by the solemnity of his theme, might be expected to speak. His voice was a volume of sweet, full, natural sound, unmarked by any artistic training or modulation, and such as would flow from a well-bred man in animated recitation ; and his gestures were those which rose spontaneously and unconsciously with the thought, and were wholly unstudied ; thus presenting an obvious contrast to the manner and action of his friend Randolph, whose every attitude, the slightest motion of whose finger, the faintest intonation of whose voice, whose every smile and frown, natural as they seemed, were the deliberate reflection of the closet.

Three years later, in the Virginia Convention of 1829, I heard all that he uttered in committee and in the body ; and his manner was such as I have just described it to be. Although he had full command of the whole armory of parliamentary warfare, he had none of that violent gesticulation or loud intonation which fashion or taste has lately introduced among us, but which would not be tolerated a moment in the British House of Commons. His first speech, which was in support of his own resolution proposing a method of procedure in the discussion of the Constitution, though fine and effective, was delivered under somewhat unfavorable circumstances. He stood some distance from the Chair and on a line with it, so that he was compelled to face the audience instead of the Speaker, and to pitch his voice to a key that could be heard throughout the length of the hall and the crowded galleries, and an occasional hoarseness, the result of overstraining, was apparent during his speech. He mentioned this circumstance to me as we left the hall, as the first intimation he had of having lost that control of his voice which had hitherto been equal to every occasion. But when he followed Mr. Monroe, he happened to be in a better position on the floor ; and his voice retained its usual fulness, and was pleasing to the ear. And afterwards in the Baptist church, to which the Convention adjourned, in his speech on the election of Governor, his voice was fresh and musical ; and in the grand debate on the judiciary tenure, when the debaters were near each other and the Chair, he spoke with full command of his voice, and with great animation. In fine, his manner, including the management of his voice and gesture, approached nearer the English model of debating than that which has been gradually gaining ground in this country, and was most appropriate to his style of thought and discussion.

Tazewell, with all his intercourse with the world, with all his habits of speaking, and with all his marvellous endowments, was a remarkably modest man. His modesty may unfold a clew to the explanation of his whole career. He said himself that he never rose to make a speech without serious trepidation. In the cochineal case, it was obvious to the court and to the spectators. I seen him have, when he had been speaking ten minutes, not fully assured. It was only when personal danger, as in a memorable criminal case, in which even brave men were for a time appalled, was present, that his trepidation disappeared, and he became fearless and defiant.

Nor was the modesty of Tazewell confined to the bar. It pervaded his whole life ; and when his fame was coëxtensive with the Union, and when his presence inspired awe in companies of able men, a close observer could detect in his tones or in his manner that he was not wholly at ease. It was only when the ice of a gathering party was fairly broken, that he was thoroughly self-possessed. Like Judge Marshall, he had a profound sense of respect for the female sex ; and his attentions to women were rendered with a delicacy and a gallantry that were enhanced by the reflection that such a man was not wholly at ease in approaching them. And nobly did woman repay his courtesy and his affection. As I dwell upon this aspect of his life, the image of her who was the bride of his youth, the partaker of his splendid fame, and the delight of his declining years, rises before me. I behold her as she moved in that happy household, bestowing not a thought upon herself, but intent on making others happy. I see her as she enters the room in which her husband is discoursing on learned topics to those who are grouped around him, and I see him pause as that " ocean-eye " rests benignantly and affectionately upon her. I shall never forget the moment when thirty-five years ago I saw her in her own house for the first time ; how cordially she pressed my hand ; how kindly she talked to an orphan boy of a father he had never known ; and how soon she put an awkward youth of seventeen at his ease. The characteristic grace of that admirable woman was her love of domestic life. With her the throne of human felicity was the family altar. Life with her, as it ever was with those elder Virginia matrons whom she resembled, was too serious a business for pomp and show. Had she been inspired with a passion for display, had she coveted the fleeting honors of a residence at a foreign court, or in the metropolis of our own country, a single word from her lips would have obtained all she wished. But her heart, like a true Virginia mother as she was, was in the midst of her family; and though she properly appreciated the talents of her husband, and was willing that they should be exerted in the public service, she knew him well, and believed that he would be happier in his own home than when he was beset with public cares, or galled by those tortures with which ambition wrings its victims. And when her last day had come, and the union of more than half a century had been dissolved, and her husband had seen her beloved remains put away in that solitary tomb by the sea, the charm of life was lost to him; and he calmly awaited the hour when he should be laid by her side. Nor did the generous care of woman cease with her death. When his hour was come, and he was placed beside her, his daughters, who had tended him for years with unceasing devotion, were borne in almost a dying state from his tomb.

He was keenly alive to the pleasures of friendship; and he maintained his affection for his early schoolmates unbroken to the last. His reverence for Mr. Wythe passed all words. Randolph loved him through life; and Tazewell reciprocated his affection with equal warmth. The tide of his affection for John Wickham from his childhood flowed full and strong. The relations which existed between them could be seen in the letter I read some time ago, and were earnest, tender, and affectionate. The affection which Tazewell cherished for Wickham, kindled, as we have seen, over the spelling-book and the Latin grammar, and showing itself in tears in his sixty-fifth year, grew with his growth, and was enhanced by that elevated sense of appreciation with which each regarded the other. It was pleasing to see them together when the descending shadows of age were upon them, and when each had performed those deeds which are now deemed the greatest of their lives. It would be hard to say whether they stood to each other in the relation of father and son, of brothers, or of equals. Wickham was eleven years older than Tazewell, and had taught him to read. It was evident Mr. Tazewell regarded Mr. Wickham with the greatest deference. It was, however, something more than the deference with which one eminent man advanced in life would show to another eminent man still more advanced; it was the deference of the warmest friendship to an individual who not only reciprocated the feelings of affection, but who possessed all the moral and intellectual qualities that can adorn human nature. He considered Mr. Wickham not only the most accomplished lawyer this country ever produced, but the wisest man he ever knew. I have heard him say that the speech of Mr. Wickham on the doctrine of treason in Burr's trial would have been pronounced new and able in Westminster Hall; and that it was the greatest forensic effort of the American bar. Tazewell's abiding affection for Wickham was such, that he drew upon it in favor even of his young friends. When, at one-and-twenty, I took my seat in the House of Delegates, and, not dreaming of mixing in society, was preparing for a course of study during the long winter nights, one of the first calls I received was from Mr. Wickham. With me his name had passed into history. His great speech, which I had read and studied as I had read and studied the speeches of Chatham and of Burke, was made in the year I was born. But I soon found that he was a living and breathing man. His gentle kindness, his incomparable address, his charming talk, and his cordial hospitality pressed upon me, assured me that his heart still glowed with its ancient kindness: and when I recall the hours which I spent at his elegant home; when I recollect the names of Marshall, Leigh, Johnson, Stanard, Harvie, and others whom I have seen at his hospitable board; when I recall that living galaxy of beauty which flashed in his thronged halls, and of which the sweetest and the brightest were his own household stars,—now, alas! extinct and gone; and his own noble presence and demeanor, which drew from the spoiled and fastidious poet Moore the expression of his admiration and applause, it is with feelings of deep and tender regard, and of grateful veneration, that I offer this tribute to his memory.

The question has often been asked whether Mr. Tazewell was fond of literature and had the elements of a literary man. His early opportunities were not favorable for acquiring a profound knowledge of classical learning. In his day Latin and Greek, the foundation of all true taste in letters, were not taught in William and Mary at all, except in the grammar school. That Tazewell knew enough of Latin to translate easily a Latin author, and even to write the language grammatically, is certain; but that he never rose to that excellence in those tongues to which his old tutor Mr. Wythe attained is equally certain. But of English literature he had drunk deeply. He had Bacon, Locke, Burke, Pope, Shakspeare, Swift, Hume, Gibbon, Johnson, Gillies, Addison, and Roscoe, within three feet of his elbow for the last forty years of his life. In English political history, such as might be gathered from the ordinary historians, and from such books as Baker's Chronicle and Rushworth, he was profoundly skilled. The history of the law from the days of Magna Charta to the passage of the reform bill of Earl Grey's administration, was the study of his whole professional and public life. He not only knew every leading event, every great statute, but he had the minutest details at command, and was always pleased to descant upon a British statute, or on an epoch of British legislation. The excellent volumes of Lord Chancellor Campbell have made a knowledge of the history of the law an easy accomplishment; but Tazewell never read them, and drew his information from the original sources. In the history of Virginia he was, without exception, the greatest proficient of his time. Whatever was told by Smith, Beverly, Keith, Stith, and Burk with his continuators, or by Hening in the statutes at large, or in the journals of the House of Burgesses and of the House of Delegates, or could be gathered from the living voice for eighty years, he knew intimately and could recall at a moment's notice. In respect of the political history of the United States from the adoption of the federal constitution to the day of his death, his knowledge was accurate, ready, and profound. Indeed, if we except the first five years of the federal constitution, it may be said that his actions were a part of that history. He had discussed, in the House of Delegates, the leading measures of the Washington and Adams administrations, and sixty years ago he sate at a stormy period in the House of Representatives of the United States.

But the excellence of Mr. Tazewell consisted not so much in knowing the acts and thoughts of other men, as in the philosophy which he drew from the great facts in all history. He was not in the German, or even in the English sense, a reader of many books; but there was hardly a topic of literature or history which he had not studied, and respecting which he had not elaborated a theory of his own. Even in law he was more apt to work out a question which required a solution than to turn to the books of reports. Neither at the bar nor in the senate was he fond of quoting authorities; but such as he did quote were of the highest merit, and he made them do him yeoman service. Burton's Anatomy of Melancholy and Warburton's Divine Legation of Moses were favorite books with him. He thought the report of John Quincy Adams on weights and measures one of the ablest works in political literature.

The tendency of his mind and character was wholly practical. Common sense was his polar star. He must be judged not as a scholar or a lawyer or a statesman merely, but as a man of business who was required to accomplish a given purpose. If that purpose was to be accomplished by writing, he took up his pen; if by speech, he rose at the bar and pleaded the case, or in the senate and made a speech. But when the end was attained he thought no more about the means which he had used in attaining it, whether by writing or speaking, than the carpenter who has finished a house thinks of the scaffolding by which he was enabled to complete it. Hence Mr. Tazewell never corrected a speech for the press, if we except two instances; and his greatest speeches are either wholly lost, or exist in the merest outline. But, looking to the result, he was almost invariably successful, at least in the sphere in which he acted; and on the attainment of his purpose forgot the means by which he reached it. If his speeches such as they are, his reports on public questions, his legal opinions, his essays and tracts on political and historical topics, and his private letters, were collected together, the variety of his powers and his singular abilities would strike every reader; and that his works ought to be preserved in volumes is a matter of public interest and is due to his memory.

I have said that Mr. Tazewell should not be considered as a mere scholar, a mere lawyer, or a mere statesman, but in that most august of all characters, the citizen of a commonwealth. But to show what manner of man he was to my younger friends, let us regard him in the aspect of a lawyer, and as he stood in the three great departments of his profession. In criminal law he was easily the first. It was the opinion of a gentleman, his early contemporary at the bar, who has united in his own person in a more eminent degree than was ever before known in Virginia the rare qualities of a writer on metaphysics, history, and literature,—an opinion expressed to me since the death of Tazewell,—that he was the ablest criminal lawyer of his age, and that he would sooner confide an important criminal case to him than to any other living man. This is but an echo of his general reputation in this department of the law. Analyze the qualities necessary to form a great criminal lawyer—his various power of speech, his skill in the evisceration of facts, his tact and ability in arranging the best line of defence possible in the case, the skill in addressing the jury, and the skill, of a different sort, in addressing the court, his superior generalship in the conflicting and unexpected developments during a trial which threaten instant defeat, his fearlessness, and that perfect self-possession which not only conceals his own fears and weaknesses, but avails itself of the fears and weaknesses of others, and of that deep insight into human passions, penetrating far beyond the eye, or the ear, or the ordinary reason: count the attainments which such a man must possess to win supremacy in such a sphere, and we must assent to the general opinion which places supremacy in such a sphere one of the highest achievements of human intellect and character. Then contemplate that excellence which is shown in the conduct of civil cases as contradistinguished from criminal —that various power here, too, of speech, in itself the lesson of a life to learn—the skill, too, in addressing juries and the court with equal effect; that knowledge of the law in its innumerable doctrines, principles, and decisions, which made the study even in Lord Coke's day the work of twenty years; the prompt application of this learning to the rapid matter in hand; the magical use of the faculties of the mind and the wondrous discipline which they must have undergone, every hour, every minute demanding a stretch of thought and an adroitness of discrimination which have justly classed the dialectics of the bar above all the dialectics of the schools; and the moral as well as intellectual qualities necessary in an adept in the varying practice of municipal law; and here, too, we will yield to the general opinion which places excellence in this single department one of the highest achievements of mind; and then recall what such a judge as Spencer Roane, the ablest and sternest judge of the age, and politically hostile to Tazewell, said when Tazewell pleaded the case of Long *vs.* Colston before the Court of Appeals. Then let us follow the profession beyond and above the region of municipal law into the higher walk of the Laws of Nations, and of that great practical part of those laws, the law of admiralty. Consider what eminence is, and what it involves, in this department which the master spirits of ancient as well as of modern time selected as their peculiar sphere; what the talents are that may contend with the greatest intellects of the age in that greatest of all our gladiatorial arenas, the Supreme Court of the United States, and what various and rare excellencies must unite in forming a man who may stand forth and share in such generous battle, and, still more, shall come off victorious from such a field. And when, by blending all these characters, each great in itself, and worthy of the ambition of the highest talents and of the longest life, into a single character, we have made a fame which the grandest intellects of modern times might glory in attaining, we have but one of the elements, developed during a comparatively short period only of his career, that make up the reputation of him whose memory we have met this day to honor.

Then, if you please, regard him as a senator, representing the sovereignty of Virginia in our more than Amphictyonic Council. Take any speech which he delivered during his term of service—the speech on the Bankrupt law; the speech on the Piracy bill, which, as it was delivered by him, and not as it appears debased and dwarfed in the report, was one of the grandest displays of pure intellect ever made in the Senate, and which saved the country from giving cause of war to Spain and, perhaps and probably, from actual war; the speech on the Census, which his colleague who sat by his side during its delivery told me gave both Calhoun and Webster quite as much to do as was grateful to both of them; the speech on the Admirals; the reports from the Committee on Foreign Affairs for seven or eight years which controlled the public opinion of the time; that consummate ability which in its grandest displays inspired the hearer with the belief that the speaker, great as he was, was capable of yet greater things—*par negotiis et supra*—his speeches so settling matters that it seemed almost vain to say anything after him for or against, and calling the remark from Webster, when Tazewell was making one of his last speeches in the senate, " Why, Tazewell grows greater every day." Form your notion of what must enter into the formation of such a character, and then you have another of those elements that make up the character of Tazewell.

Then take your model of a man who draws his sustenance from the plough, a private citizen, who lives privately, not because he cannot obtain office, but because, having won the highest honors, he withdraws from the scene and leaves the glittering rewards of public service to be divided among those who seek them. Look for his name in the newspapers, and you will not find it from year's end to year's end ; look for deep intrigues in local politics, and you will find no finger of his in the dirty work. Look at the ill success of those who have engaged in public affairs, their pecuniary entanglements, their deferred hopes, their sleepless nights, those poisoned fountains of feeling bitter as aloes even to the eye that looks on them as they bubble ; these and such things you may find, and find easily, but not at the door of Tazewell. He is strictly a private citizen, engaged in his private affairs, raising and selling at fair prices in company with his neighbors his oats and corn and potatoes, and showing to all that the highest faculties are as practical as the lowest, and that diligence and attention always have their reward. Without patrimony, with a moderation in taking fees without an example in our land, living as became a gentleman of his position in life and affairs, he yet accumulated a larger fortune than was probably ever before accumulated by a Virginia farmer or a lawyer beginning life without patrimony ; and when wealth was obtained, living with that modesty and simplicity so becoming to great genius and great wealth, ever looking with just contempt on that most piteous of all spectacles, the spectacle of lofty genius debruised and debased by the accursed thirst for gold ; and presenting in all the private relations of life an example which may be held up for the imitation of the old and the young. When you have combined these various characters into one whole, you may form some general notion of what Mr. Tazewell was.

His head was of the clearest. Horace says of Apollo that he did not always keep his bow bent ; but Tazewell's mind was always on the stretch, or, in a stricter sense, was never on the stretch at all. The most intricate combination of figures he saw through at a glance; and in the arts the most complex machinery was easily understood by him, and readily made plain to others by his familiar explanations. Processes of reasoning the most elaborate seemed rather the play of his mind than a serious exercise of its powers; and in his most refined speculations he never for a moment lost himself, or allowed the hearer to lose him. When in a playful mood he chose to use the weapons of the sophist, the ablest men feared the ticklish game and fought shy; and where the line lay between truth and error it was impossible to find out; and he was equally skilful in unravelling the sophistry of others, dissecting it asunder with the keenest relish and with exquisite skill. When he seriously undertook to assert and defend the truth, he was irresistible, and it was vain to oppose him. Excessive ingenuity has been laid at his door; but, while conceding that his long dallying with inferior courts was likely to lead to faults in that direction, yet, if we look to the occasions when he was charged with using it, and its effect at the time, we may be inclined to believe that his judgment of the line of argument to be pursued was as likely to be appropriate as that of the critic who formed his opinion according to some abstract standard of propriety.

He was never out of tune. Call on him when you would, and you found him self-poised and fresh. Argument or narrative followed at your command. This part of his character was very apparent to me during the last seven years of his life. In that interval I called to see him frequently; and, as my own studies lay in the walks of our earlier history, the talk usually ran, for a time at least, on the men and things of an epoch in which the Revolution held the middle place. He seemed to have perfect command of his stores, not by the mere effort of recollection, but of memory and reflection combined, eliminating a truth from the facts which concealed it. A specimen of the talk which actually occurred between us may illustrate my remark. I would approach him and say deliberately in his ear—for within a few years past he had become slightly deaf—"Mr. Tazewell, Col. Richard Bland (who, by the way, died in October, 1776) wrote tracts in the Parson's cause, a tract against the Quakers, and his inquiry into the rights of the colonies; did he write any other pamphlet?"

Quick as thought he replied : "Yes, he wrote a tract on the tenure of lands in Virginia, showing that they were allodial and not held in fee. I read the tract when I was a boy ; and it helped me in in my examination for a license to practise law." He had probably not recalled this fact before for half a century : no copy of the tract is preserved ; and there was not another human being then living, I may venture to say, who knew of the existence of such a tract ; and so at times with other facts which he recalled after the lapse of seventy years, and which he had learned from his father or from Mr. Wythe. On the other hand, when his earlier recollections were clearly proved to be inaccurate as to matter of fact, as in the case of what he thought had happened at the session of the House of Burgesses of 1765, when Henry's resolutions against the stamp act were passed, and I placed under his eye the discrepancy between his statement of the case and the entry on the journals of the House, he would fight manfully in defence of his own views, but generally ended in cases where the proof was conclusive : "Well, sir, Mr. Wythe told me so." Dates not common or easily reached were fixed in his memory by a kind of connexion with his own life ; as for instance, I would ask him whether he remembered the features of Peyton Randolph ? And he would answer : "No, sir ; I was born in December, 1774, and he died in October, 1775, in Philadelphia, when I was not a year old." And it was by questions such as these, which I could answer with exact precision myself, that I ascertained not only the integrity and worth of his memory, which we all know in aged persons retains with freshness the incidents of youth, but his capacity of combination which, in the degree in which he possessed it, was extremely rare in young or old ; and from the nature of my pursuits for the time in question I may be said not only to have tested his powers of recollection, but to have probed the depth of his knowledge in relation to the history of Virginia and its cognate topics more effectually than it was the privilege of any one else to do ; and my admiration of his talents and of his resources increased to the last. Let it be remembered that there was no more reason to look for profound learning on these subjects from Mr. Tazewell, whose life was crowded with business, than from any of his eminent contemporaries, some of whom I knew well, but none of whom approached him in these respects ; and I have pointed out, merely for the sake of example, a single department of knowledge only in which I happened to take a passing interest, leaving all those untouched on which I have heard him discourse for thirty years at least, and you will be able to form an opinion of the nature, variety, and extent of his acquisitions, and feel with me what a gap the death of such a man has made in the commonwealth.

From the complexion of his mind he was cautious in bestowing commendation on men and things. Great speeches in public bodies rarely came up to his severe and simple standard of taste ; and I do not think that he was sensible in a very high degree of the minor elegancies of rhythm and the harmony of words. His own style might be defined plain words in their right places ; and he had studied Anglo-Saxon, and drew largely on the Anglo-Saxon element of our tongue, and especially on its monosyllables. His logic was generally so severe that not a clause and hardly a word could be changed or misplaced without danger, and the merit of his work was rather in the strength and beauty of the demonstration as a whole, than in the rhetorical grace or effect of its several parts. I speak of his great arguments. In his letters he sometimes showed a skill in harmony rarely surpassed. His letter to the executor of Mr. Wickham is delicately drawn ; his letter to Mr. Foote on the compromise resolutions is a chaste and elegant composition ; and his address from the chair at a meeting of the citizens of Norfolk on the occasion of the death of Jefferson, which I have already alluded to, when he proposed a statue to the author of the Declaration of Independence, was of that rare beauty of thoughts and words in happy union bound, that, though delivered thirty-four years ago, it is with me to this hour one of the most refreshing of my memories of the past. But these were exceptions, and his severe standard was the general rule. Hence, while he valued the vast and conclusive learning of Gibbon, he was not taken with his diction ; and though he despised the toryism of Hume, he regarded his style as approaching perfection. He liked the fervid genius of the elder Pitt, and his brilliant speeches, because they were effective weapons in their day ; but he would look with contempt at any effort of imitation. While he relished the arguments of Judge Marshall at the bar, in public bodies, and on the bench, I do not think that he placed as high a value as they deserved upon the ability and literary taste which characterize the opinions of Judge Story, and which have earned for their author the highest legal fame at home and abroad. From the eloquent parts of such speeches as Webster's in reply to Hayne he would turn with dislike. Yet when a speech was effective in the delivery, and, though not remarkable in itself, had accomplished something, he was liberal in bestowing fair praise upon it. He heard Mr. Clay deliver his celebrated reply to Josiah Quincy—a venerable statesman who still survives;—and he ever spoke of it as admirable in its way. In the same spirit he spoke of Col. Benton's extemporaneous reply to Mr. Webster in the debate on the bank veto, delivered late at night in the Senate, as surpassing any thing of the kind that he had ever heard, or that the speaker ever reached before or after. He said he thought a speech of Webster's delivered during the war or soon after it, probably the speech on the currency, superior to his speech in reply to Hayne, and altogether free from the tinsel of his later speeches. The speech of Pinkney on the Missouri question, which he heard, he thought the ablest ever delivered in the senate. For the intellect of Calhoun he had the highest respect and admiration, and, while differing most essentially from that statesman throughout nearly his whole career, he always regarded his speeches and state papers as those of a master-workman. Strange as it may appear, though exacting so much from his eminent contemporaries, yet, partly from old affection, partly from a love of their literature and from a conviction of their political effect, and partly from the unworthiness of poor human nature, he listened to the speeches of John Randolph with the relish of a school-boy, rubbing his hands and laughing heartily as the orator went along. Aside from the ardent and unquenchable love that existed between them, the explanation may be found to a certain extent in Tazewell's love of humor. When Watkins Leigh's amusing letter of Christopher Quandary appeared in the Enquirer,—a paper, by the way, which, after the feud in the Jefferson administration, he never took in, thus showing that, if the democrats remembered his shortcomings, he did not forget what he deemed theirs—I took the number around to him, and he laughed heartily at its hits. The last extended work which I know that he read was Randall's Life of Jefferson, which evidently made an impression upon him. He spoke of the author as a clever fellow ; and he expatiated on the character of Jefferson, which, as he declined in life, I think he valued more than ever, pronouncing him the greatest Secretary of State any country ever had. I may say here, that Mr. Tazewell had no respect for law schools as an instrumentality of rearing great lawyers. He said if the student would have lectures, let him read Blackstone ; and he ever maintained the opinion that the popularity of those charming commentaries had tended to depreciate the standard of legal intellect since their appearance—an opinion which he shared with Mr. Jefferson. That he had read them attentively and admired their beauty, though much in the spirit in which he would admire a poem or a play, I know from this fact, that once, when he was in a playful mood, he said he believed he could repeat the heads of all the chapters of the four volumes which he straightway did. He occasionally read novels, but was quite indifferent whether he began with the second or the first volume ; and I heard him commend highly the preface of the late novel attributed to Sir Walter Scott, called Moredun, as a fine piece of special pleading, declaring that its author would make a good special pleader. I have spoken already of the hearty praise which he bestowed upon Mr. Adams' report on weights and measures.

In respect both of argumentation and style it has often occurred to me that Mr. Tazewell occupied an intermediate position between Judge Marshall and Mr. Wickham. He has the strength of Marshall with something more of refinement in style and imagery, and more vivacity in the play of his reasoning ; while he has a stricter line of demonstration than Wickham without his very decided elegance. In some physical as well as intellectual aspects he resembled Chief Justice Parsons of Massachusetts. Not, indeed, in dress ; for Parsons was a sloven, and Tazewell was neat in his dress, which was in winter, during the last twenty years, a full suit of black cloth, and in summer he was usually attired in white drilling with a light linen coat and fancy vest. He always wore a white cravat, and his linen was spotless. But both Parsons and Tazewell were men of large stature, at least to the eye, in a sitting posture ; both delighted to drink at the deep fountains of the law, and were skilled in the lore of their profession in which they held an easy supremacy ; both liked novels as a relief from grave cares, and were indifferent as to the volume of the novel that first came to hand ; both were so strongly enamored of the exact sciences that it is probable they would have cultivated them with extraordinary success. But Tazewell, though a fair scholar in the old way, never attained to that excellence in classical literature which made the name of Parsons an authority for a disputed reading in the colleges of Germany. I have always regretted that Tazewell did not bring his mind to bear upon the science of language, and especially of comparative philology. Had he been able to read Bonn, or had mastered the New Cratylus or the Varronianus of Donaldson, his versatile and sharp intellect might have sent forth a work of " winged words " of equal interest and infinitely more profound than the Diversions of Purley.

Tazewell had evidently modelled his mind before the death of president Pendleton in 1802 ; and nearly up to that period Marshall and Wickham were the leaders of the Virginia bar. His reverence for Pendleton was something more than a shadow. It was, as also in the case of Wythe, a deep-seated, ever-living and glowing principle. He loved those two illustrious judges with a warmth of veneration blended with affection which he never felt for any human being after they were laid in their graves ; and he delighted to speak of them. He held Pendleton's judicial talents in the highest respect ; and I have heard him say that no man living but Pendleton could have reconciled the clashing laws passed during the first twelve years of the commonwealth, and made such just and satisfactory decisions. Speaking of the peculiarities of Pendleton and Wythe, he said that Pendleton always professed the most profound respect for British decisions, but rarely followed them ; while Wythe, who spoke disrespectfully of them, almost invariably followed them. But, on the ground of pure love and affection, Wythe was nearer to Tazewell than was Pendleton. Wythe was the guide and instructor of his youth, the old neighbor of his father in Williamsburg ; and he always spoke of him as *Mr.* Wythe, following his father who knew Wythe long before he was a judge. His reminiscences of Wythe were deeply interesting, sometimes humorous, sometimes serious, and, in reference to the last illness of the old patriot, sad in the extreme; and they were always uttered in that subdued and tender tone which, it grieves me to think, will fall no more on mortal ears.

The great age attained by Mr. Tazewell makes us curious to know his modes of life and his habits of study. In youth and early manhood he was fond of athletic sports and of horsemanship; and he must have possessed great muscular power. As late as 1802 he accomplished on horseback a trip of a hundred and odd miles in as short a time as that distance was ever travelled in Virginia. His form was most symmetrical; and he had the broad chest and the well-proportioned neck that are so often seen in those who enjoy a healthful and protracted old age; and that small wrist and hand that told of his Norman blood. From the time when he became engrossed in business, it is probable that he rarely took any other exercise than was inevitable in passing to his various courts; and since his retirement from the bar, except during his trips to the Eastern Shore and to Washington and Richmond, he seldom walked more than a few hundred yards in twenty-four hours. Yet, throughout his career, he enjoyed fair health, and during the last forty years, when, as man and boy, I have observed him, he has not had more than one really serious spell of illness—a pleuritic attack, which he encountered in Washington. In that interval he has contracted several bilious diseases; but they soon passed off, and were not thought dangerous. The secret of his exemption from disease, apart from the healthful structure of his frame, was the extreme temperance and the regularity of his habits. At first sight he would seem the most irregular of men, sitting up till two or three in the morning and rising late; but, in fact, this habit, persisted in for so many years, became fixed; and, as nature requires regular periods of rest rather than any special time for taking it, he suffered no material inconvenience in that respect. But his main source of exemption from sickness was his temperance in eating. I had an opportunity of seeing him daily at every meal for many weeks, and he ate more sparingly than any one of those who sate at the table with him. He generally took a glass of toddy or a glass of wine at dinner; and the only form in which he used tobacco was in chewing. If he ever went into excess in any thing it was in the use of tobacco; but he never appeared to me to err above ordinary chewers even in that way, though I have heard one of his clerks say that he could always tell the dignity of a case by the size of the chew which Tazewell put into his mouth when he took it up for the first time. His usual remedy for indisposition was strict abstinence from food, which he could endure as heroically as a Brahmin, or a disciple of Mahomet.

Many to whom the name of Mr. Tazewell is dear would be inclined to know his opinion respecting the religion of Christ. Far be it from me to intimate in the remotest degree that the testimony of any man, however distinguished, can add the weight of a single feather to the abounding evidences of the Christian faith, or grave it a line deeper on the heart of a true believer; but it may close the lips of the ribald, it may repress the vanity of her who, forgetting what Christianity has done for woman, aims her feeble shafts against its humblest professor, to know that such a man as Tazewell, whose whole life was spent in the science of proofs and probabilities, must henceforth be ranked with Milton and Newton—the prince of song and the prince of philosophy, and with our own Pendleton and Wythe—those serene and undying lights of the law—among the stedfast believers in the truth of the Scriptures of the Old and New Testaments.*

It has been said that Tazewell had no ambition. In one sense he was the most ambitious man of our times; but his ambition was out of the ordinary range. To retain a seat in a deliberative assembly, and endure the routine of daily sessions for months at a time; to take upon himself a regular foreign mission, or even to accept the presidency itself, would, I firmly believe, have been most grating to his feelings. Of all but the last we may speak with certainty. But if some difficult proposition was forced upon the public mind; if some extraordinary emergency had presented itself; if he had been called upon to encounter a national question of the first magnitude, from which others would have shrunk, and which was susceptible of a definitive adjustment in a given time, I believe he would have accepted the mission at once. Had Mr.

* In a note to a friend, written Christmas day, 1850, he speaks of the Bible as "the good book," and says, "it has ever been regarded as most precious."

Madison, on his election to the presidency, called him to the State Department with a *carte blanche* as to the terms and mode of settling the vexed questions which grew out of the Berlin and Milan decrees and the British orders in council, I do not say that he would have accepted a seat in the cabinet of a statesman whose election to the presidency he had opposed,—for I believe he would not; but, if he had accepted it, it is probable those questions which were afterwards discussed by Mr. Webster and Lord Ashburton, and which were settled by the treaty of Washington, would then have received a satisfactory solution. It was this aspect of Tazewell's character which called from Randolph the saying in his letter to Gen. Mercer, that, if such a conjuncture in our affairs were to arise as would call into full play the faculties of Tazewell, he would be the first man of the nineteenth century.

It has been said by some from whom better things might have been expected, that Tazewell did not spend his latter years in a manner altogether worthy of his great talents. To me it appears that such a sentiment has been expressed without due reflection on all the facts of the case, and that the retirement of such a man, under all the circumstances, presents to the contemplative observer one of the grandest moral spectacles of the age. We have seen that he retired from the active employment of the bar in his 45th or 46th year, merely following up afterwards to the appellate courts some important cases which he had discussed in the lower. At that time he stood almost without a rival in his profession in Virginia, and, after the death of Pinkney, in the Supreme Court of the United States; and he might have received as large an annual income as was ever derived from the practice of the law in this country; and if he had devoted his time and talents to his profession for twenty years thereafter—which he might have done, and yet been younger on leaving off than Webster was when that eminent lawyer pleaded the great India-rubber case at Trenton, and would still have had sixteen or eighteen years to spare for repose in old age,—he would have accumulated the most colossal fortune which has ever been made by forensic exertions at the American or the English bar. Now this very aspect of the life of Mr. Tazewell strikes me, and I feel assured will appear to posterity, as the most imposing, the most eloquent, and the most sublime picture in his various career. When he retired he was not wealthy, according to our present standard of wealth, and he had several children born to him after his retirement; yet, with enormous wealth within his grasp, and a moderate competency only in hand, he withdrew from the field of his fame to the bosom of his family, thenceforth to draw his living from the moderate profits of agriculture. I have said that Mr. Tazewell's character was formed in the mould of our early statesmen; and of all those statesmen there was not one who did not delight in agriculture as the crowning pleasure and pursuit of life, and more especially as its shadows were falling low. It was this spirit which impelled Washington, amid all the magnificence of office when office was held by such a man, to sigh for the shades of Mount Vernon, and to prefer the simple employments of the farm, where he might behold, in the words of the "judicious Hooker," "God's blessing spring out of our mother earth," above the glory of arms, and the fleeting shadows and shabby splendors of public office.

But the lesson which the example of Tazewell presents to the American mind is of yet greater significancy. If there be one unpleasant trait more revolting than another in our national character, it is the inordinate pursuit of wealth: *rem, quocunque modo rem.* To get money is the first lesson of childhood, the engrossing purpose of middle age, and the harassing employment of declining years. Such is the rabid thirst for money, its effects are seen over the whole moral and intellectual character of the people. It constitutes wealth as the standard of worth, and all the noblest qualities of the head and the heart are despised in the comparison. As wealth is the point of honor, it must be sought at every hazard, and the mortifying occurrences of the last twenty years, the dishonest bankruptcies, the numerous forgeries, perpetrated by the first people in social position, on a scale never known before, the innumerable defalcations which have crowded the papers, until they have become a matter of course; the insatiable craving for the money and lands of others, which seems to have passed from the workshop and the counting-room to the halls of legislation; the unbounded extravagance of expenditure which might serve to indicate the possession of the darling prize, and, above all, that worst sign of all, the almost perfect indifference with which the most enormous frauds are received by the public; these and similar things show the bitter consequences of this vulgar passion. I rejoice that our venerable friend, when in the prime of his extraordinary powers, and at a period of life when the flame of ambition glows wildest, turned his back upon the gilded phantoms which have lured so many to destruction, and sought repose in the bosom of domestic life.

The conduct of Mr. Tazewell in respect of public office has also been misunderstood. He would hold no office in perpetuity, and I have already shown that, whenever called upon to render public service, he obeyed the call without a thought of the pecuniary sacrifices which he inevitably must incur;* and it would be easy, if it were proper, to show that Mr. Tazewell, though in retirement, afforded most valuable assistance to those who held office, and indeed to all who chose to consult him. He held it as a settled maxim, that it was the first duty of every citizen to serve his country; and I have no doubt that, if the office of Chief Justice of the United States had become vacant during the first fifteen or twenty years after his retirement from the bar, and he had been called to fill it, as perhaps he would have been, he would have accepted the appointment; and I further believe that if the presidency of the Court of Appeals had been tendered him, or even the judgeship of the Superior Court on the Eastern Shore, provided in this last case he did not interfere with the expectations of his brethren of that bar, he would have accepted either, and held it for a certain time, and for a certain time only; for he had no respect for perpetuities in great public trusts.

They also misjudge him who say that he ought to have composed a great historical work for posterity—a task which Jefferson, Madison, and John Quincy Adams, with every possible motive urging them to its performance, declined to undertake. In this respect, Mr. Tazewell acted with his usual good sense; not that he did not write on particular topics of our history, as, for instance,

* From letters in my possession, I could quote a dozen instances in which he expresses his readiness to accept any office which the State might confer upon him; but he did not desire any appointment State or Federal; that he would seek none, but that he could not refuse his services to Virginia when she required them. See extracts in Appendix, No. 4.

the difference between the original and recent surveys, a subject which he has illustrated with a skill in mathematics, with a beauty of argumentation, and with a minuteness of historical research wholly unexpected, and altogether admirable; and so with some other topics. But he acted well in not undertaking the history of Virginia. To write that history worthily would require a residence of some years abroad. Of the materials necessary for such a work not a twentieth part exists in Virginia, or in the United States. Such a work, and Mr. Tazewell well knew its scope, could not be performed by him in that retirement to enjoy which he had relinquished wealth and fame. There is another view of a more personal kind. Whether history is of higher dignity than speech, whether a Thucydides or a Demosthenes be the greater intellect, the critics may decide; but one thing is certain, that the faculties and accomplishments required for writing history and for oral disputations are not only not the same, but have rarely been united in a supreme degree in any human being, and certainly not in the literature of the Anglo-Saxon race. To pass over other languages and nations, let us look at our own. One of the greatest minds of this age, and, so far as logical capacity is concerned, perhaps of any age, was that of Chief Justice Marshall; and yet, from the date of the publication of his Life of Washington, which is a history of the colonies and of the United States, until it was re-written and revised by him late in life, it hung like a millstone from his neck; and it has required all his subsequent legal fame, his exalted patriotism, and his domestic purity, to keep him above water in this country. As for England, the work sunk instantly and irrecoverably.

The writing of history, difficult at all times, is more difficult now. Recent history trenches alike upon the epic and the dramatic, and the narrator must be half a poet and half a player. It is, therefore, a subject of gratulation that Mr. Tazewell did not undertake a work which, if done at home, would have been badly done, and which, if done at all, must have called into exercise a peculiar class of talents which neither the bar nor the senate tends to develop, but which in their highest efforts alone can ensure success. I rejoice that the fame of Tazewell is free from such questionable topics. There he stands, great as a citizen of a free commonwealth, great at the bar, great in the senate, and great in his rich, various, and overflowing talk.

Tazewell spent his old age as Washington, Jefferson, Jay, Madison, and John Adams spent theirs, but with far greater success than them all, in attending mainly to his private affairs, and in those offices which a splendid reputation draws in its train. He was exact in all things. If you inquired what any one of his estates cost him, he would take down a bound foolscap volume, turn at once to the farm in question, read off the price, the amount of its outfit, the number of hands engaged in working it, and, if you pleased to listen, the cost of every improvement he put upon it, the division of its fields, and their products for every year since he owned it, and the money value of those products in market. He knew what fields on his various estates were in cultivation; and in the spring—for all his crops were annual—he made an estimate of the probable product of each field, and entered it in the book; and in the fall, the actual result, which sometimes fell a little short, sometimes slightly exceeded, and sometimes was identical with the estimate of the spring. This process was something more than a pastime; it kept him intimately acquainted with his different estates, and was a severe check on the management of the overseers. He loved the game of chess, was always ready to engage in it, and often played alone. He read chess periodicals, kept an account of his own moves, and, deducting the employment which it gave him when his eyes were dimmed with reading, devoted to that fascinating but frivolous game more time and attention than it deserved.

To form a just opinion of Mr. Tazewell in private life, he must have been seen again and again. In matters of business he was scrupulously exact himself, and would be satisfied with nothing less from others. In this way he may have given offence, and subjected himself to the charge of closeness; but it was partly the result of his legal habits, and partly of the rigid system which pervaded his financial schemes. That the love of accumulation was no element in the case was shown, apart from the great lesson which his life will read to all, by his large deposits in the vaults of the banks, by which, in the course of thirty years, he must have lost thousands; and by the proverbial moderation of his fees.* Such was

* One case occurs to me. The captain of a French ship with a valuable cargo, hav-

his care and judgment that I do not think he ever made a bad investment, or lost a sum of money.

Withal I am inclined to wish that he had devoted the first ten years of his retirement to a work on the Laws of Nations, and especially of the Law of Admiralty, which was the favorite science of his venerable grandfather, and of which, during the preceding twenty years, he had obtained so perfect a mastery. He loved the Common Law, revelled in its subtleties, expounded with a richness and a grace ever to be remembered the leading statutes by which the wisdom of a thousand years had controlled or modified it, and gloried in it as the living remembrancer of the liberties of his ancestral land. But he regarded the law of admiralty with peculiar and almost hereditary affection. It suited the caste of his intellect. No ordinary horizon bounded its sphere. It overlooked the limits of any single realm, however proud that realm might seem. It was the queen of the sea, whose influence, cast far and wide over the raging billows, breathed peace and safety to the humblest sailor who trod a deck, and upheld with all the strength of civilized man the flag of the feeblest power. Amid the changing revolutions of the human will, amid the fall of empires and the ruin of dynasties, it alone was immutable. It was the tie of nations, which bound men in one universal brotherhood, and gathered peoples about a common altar. No private rule, no immemorial custom, no formal statute, controlled its operations; but right reason in all its supremacy enacted its provisions, and justice, with an even hand, in every dominion and on every sea under heaven, was its pure and equal administrator. Tazewell was fond of repeating that eloquent and exact definition of the general law, which Lord Mansfield, plucking it from the fragments of Cicero's work on the Republic, has made the household thought of our common nature: *Non erit alia lex Romæ, alia Athenis, alia nunc, alia posthac, sed et apud om-*

ing been deceived by some intelligence about the raising of the embargo, sailed into the port of Norfolk, and subjected his ship and cargo to forfeiture. Tazewell got the ship clear; and when he was informed by the consignee of the ship that the captain had left him a fee of a thousand dollars, and required his receipt for that sum, Tazewell would only accept of three hundred dollars. I may also state that when he retired from the bar, he had several thousand dollars on his books which could have been collected on application to the parties, but, whether from inadvertence or procrastination, or mere indisposition, he let them pass.

*nes gentes et omnia tempora, una eademque lex obtinebit.** Such a science suited the complexion of Tazewell's genius; and in his practice he had framed a large and liberal system of his own. The task would have been a work of love, and would have required little more than the embodiment of his thoughts on paper. But the engagements and associations of Southern life are hostile to authorship, and the fortunate time glided by forever.

A hundred years hence, when Norfolk may or may not have become the commercial seat of a vast Southern empire; when the face of external nature in this low region, unmarked by mountain ranges, will be wholly changed in all but in the course of our great river and of our two glorious seas; and when the rising genius of Virginia, turning from the sages and statesmen of Greece and Rome, from Socrates and Demosthenes, and from Cato and Cincinnatus, shall seek to know the details of the lives of the greater men who have adorned our own annals; it may be pleasing to know the spot in which Tazewell spent his latter years, and the manner of his private life. Simplicity marked his dress, his dwelling and its furniture, and all his accompaniments. His house and grounds were such as appeared, if you looked into the assessors' books, of considerable value; but if you looked at the objects themselves, they were such as any respectable citizen might possess without the reputation of great wealth. The lot, bounded on the east by Granby street, included several acres in the heart of the city; and the house, which, though capacious, had no idle room, was a plain structure of wood built originally by a private citizen of moderate means as his abode. Its position in front of a large lawn overlooking the Elizabeth could not be surpassed. The water came rippling up to the southern enclosure twice a day from the sea, and presented a broad silvery expanse on which every arriving and departing vessel of the port was borne in broad view from the portico. But, aside from the assessed value of the lot, which was accidental and produced nothing, there was no exhibition of wealth within. All was plain as became the residence of a man who had those claims to public respect which no mere wealth could give, and which the absence of wealth could not impair. As you lifted

* Luke et al. *vs.* Lyde, 2 Burrow, 887.

the knocker of his door—for he never adopted the comparative novelty of bells in our region—a black servant, who, with his ancestors of several generations, had been born in the family, soon appeared, and you entered a broad central passage which extended through the house, which was the old sitting place of Virginia families for nine months of the year, and which is hardly known in the crowded cities of the North. The floor of the passage was covered with a strip of carpeting in winter, and in summer presented a smooth polished surface devoid of matting. If you opened the first door on the left, you entered the office of Mr. Tazewell, a well lighted southern room, fourteen by twenty, in the middle of which was a table furnished with writing apparatus and covered with books and manuscripts. By that table, in an arm-chair, he commonly sate in cold weather ; and the chances were, at least during the morning, you would find him pen in hand, and sheets of paper freshly written and full of figures strewn about him. It was rare that you saw any thing like continuous writing except in the case of a letter. He delighted in calculations, which kept his mind sweet and clear. At his left hand, and a little behind him, was a small bookcase containing about two hundred volumes, neatly bound, of the English classics, all printed forty years ago and more, the very pith and quintessence of the philosophy, the politics, the literature of all ages strained through the alembic of the Anglo-Saxon mind. The office opened by a large folding-door into the capacious dining-room where the family usually sate, and where he lingered after each meal, talking, or reading the day's paper, which he took in to the last, as if loth to retire to his own particular den. In summer he sate in the passage, or on the broad tessellated pavement of the portico. On the right hand on entering the front door you saw a small room in which an aged or invalid guest might repose without ascending the stairway, and in which Gen. Jackson and Mr. Randolph lodged at various times. And adjoining this room was the parlor, a single room of twenty by twenty, containing probably the same furniture he purchased when he first went to housekeeping, all plain now, though elegant in its day, and thoroughly kept ; and suspended from the walls of the room were the portraits of his father, Judge Tazewell, a handsome youth of one-and-twenty though a married man at that age, and his bride, a sweet face almost perfectly reflected in the features of one of his own daughters, both well executed by the elder Peale, and in good preservation. There, too, were the portraits of Col. Nivison and his wife, the parents of Mrs. Tazewell; of Mr. Tazewell himself by Thompson, the most intellectual and lifelike of all his portraits, taken at the age of forty-two; of his wife's two sisters, who were the beauties and the belles of forty-five years ago, and who have long passed away, and of their brother, the amiable and beloved William Nivison, whose early death was long deplored by our people. The general library of Mr. Tazewell was kept in a separate building, and consisted of his numerous law books, of the British statutes at large in many thick quartos, and most of the writers of Queen Anne's time and of the Georges, many in the original quarto, and few or none later than the beginning of the century. Some of the books had a history of their own. There was a copy of the Lectures on History, which Dr. Priestley had presented to Judge Tazewell, the father of our subject, in memory of the kindness of the judge to the author when he was flying from the flames of Birmingham. The beautiful copy of Wilson's Ornithology with Bonaparte's continuation, which at the date of its publication was one of the most elegânt issues of the American press, had a singular value in the eyes of Mr. Tazewell as the bequest of his friend John Wickham, an extract from the will having been pasted on the fly-leaf of the first volume.

As soon as the visitor fixed his eyes on Mr. Tazewell all else was forgotten. He was without exception in middle life the most imposing, and in old age the most venerable person I ever beheld. His height exceeded six feet; and until recently, whether sitting or standing, he was commonly erect, and always when in full flow. His head and chest were on a large scale, and his vast blue eye, which always seemed to gaze afar, was aptly termed by Wirt an "eye of ocean." In early youth he was uncommonly handsome. In middle life he was very thin though lithe and strong, with a face the outline of which is very like that of Lord Mansfield. But for the last thirty-five years, the period during which I have been familiar with his person, all those traces of early beauty which had marked his youthful face, and which in middle life may be seen in the portrait of Thompson, had disappeared, and he was altogether on a more developed scale. His stature had become large, his features were massive, his silver hair fell in ringlets about his neck, and his bearing was grave, and with strangers, until the ice was broken, almost stern ; and he appeared with a majesty which filled the most careless spectator with veneration and awe. And when we add to these the overshadowing reputation universally accorded him, we can readily imagine the solicitude with which the most eminent of his contemporaries approached him for the first time. But beneath the cold surface flowed a warm and cordial current of generous feeling, or, as John Randolph said to Mercer, " his ice rested on a volcano ;" and the firm grasp of the hand, the ready talk on any topic of the time, the quick illustration which was so frequently borrowed from some characteristic or incident in the life of the person, or the person's ancestor, with whom he was conversing, the eloquent disquisition playful or profound, put the visitor at his ease, and hours flew like minutes in refreshing talk. It was a mistake to suppose that Mr. Tazewell arrogated all the talk to himself, and purposely kept others silent in his company. On the contrary, he delighted in colloquial discourse, and listened with rapt attention to all that was said ; and was then more brilliant and entertaining than ever in argument, or narrative, or repartee ; and on such occasions he was a most instructive and entertaining companion. I remember his encountering at dinner-table several gallant captains of the navy on the subject of the movements of a ship under certain relations of wind and tide ; and although the naval gentlemen combated his position with much boldness and skill, he worked his ship, at least in the opinion of the landsmen who were present, safely into her destined harbor. It was from the fear which even able men felt in his presence, and which made them averse to venture their remarks, that from pure good nature Mr. Tazewell sought to entertain and instruct them in detail on any topic of the time ; though it was plain that he courted inquiry and remark, which to a certain extent was necessary to the full and pleasant exercise of his faculties. But it was infinitely amusing to hear him banter an obstinate old lawyer on a point of law, catching at his arguments before he had half uttered them, and dissecting them with such wonderful dexterity that the listeners, shaking with laughter, saw, probably for the first time, that the severest logic and the deepest learning became in his hands the source of the keenest wit and of the broadest humor. What was conspicuous to all who had frequent opportunities of seeing Mr. Tazewell in his own house or in the house of a friend was, that he had no set topics. His range of reading and observation had been so wide, his knowledge of men and things was so vast, his faculties of combination were so active, it was impossible to state a question to be decided by precedent or reasoning, which he could not instantly handle with a force of logic which most men could only have reached by deliberate preparation. But all that humor and wit and genius are gone : that stream of talk has ceased to flow ; and on leaving the study, where for so many years he delighted his hearers by acts of personal kindness and instructed them by his wisdom, we pass into another room—the saddest of all—the chamber of Death.

There, in that room above the parlor, on the bright Sabbath morning of May the sixth, at twenty-five minutes past ten, he breathed his last. He was slightly indisposed the Monday previous ; but until the evening of that day he did not appear to be seriously ill. He complained of no particular pain, but of a general restlessness and *malaise*. On Friday, two days before his death, seated in his chair as the easiest position he could obtain, he engaged in a game of chess with a friend ; but his tremulous hand refused to make the moves, which were made by another at his suggestion, and were recorded by one of his daughters. He was too weak, however, to finish the game, which was postponed with his consent to another time. It was now plain that his disease, which was pneumonia, could not be conquered, and that his end was nigh. On Saturday morning his faculties became clouded. He was heard to call a long lost son by the name known only to the family ; then the name of his dear departed wife was uttered ; and presently the name of the master of the steamer that plies between Norfolk and the Eastern Shore where that son and that wife were buried ; showing that his own burial by their side was passing in dim review before his failing faculties. In the course of Saturday his mind was wholly gone. On Sunday morning, a quarter after ten, he drew a long breath, and it was thought that all was over ; but he rallied, and another long inspiration followed. And then all was still. His spirit had passed away. An hour later I entered the chamber, and took a seat by the side of the corpse. His hands were folded on his chest, which loomed larger than in life ; and his extended form looked like one of those marble effigies which adorn the tombs of his Norman sires. His features appeared full and natural as if a deep sleep had come upon him. The massy forehead, the firm aquiline nose, the wide reliant upper lip which looked as I have so often seen it when about to put forth a serious utterance, and the broad chin—all were there as in life ; and even his silver hair, curled freshly by a daughter's fingers, clustered about his neck and brow. The " ocean eye " alone was closed. Death had put his seal upon it. As I gazed upon that majestic form reft of its mighty spirit and soon to be laid away forever, and as I pressed the parting salutation upon those lips not yet cold in death, on which admiring Senates have so often hung, and from which I had so often heard the words of wisdom and affection, I thought of those who were bathing his dust with their tears—of the kindest and tenderest of fathers, and of the bravest and best of friends ; and I wept as I felt that a large and various chapter of my own humble life, written all over with the memories of this illustrious man,—a chapter running from early youth to grey hairs—would thenceforth be closed evermore. It was only when the flood was past, that I thought of our common country.

His time had come. He had disappeared from our sight to take his place in history. He had attained an age almost double that which his father had reached when that honored statesman fell in a distant city in the service of his country; and he had been blessed with a larger share of health than usually attends extreme old age. His faculties, which had kindled the admiration of our fathers, shone bright to the last. His children had reached maturity, and watched and cheered with tender care his failing hours ; and with each revolving morn his numerous grandchildren came with their infantile ways to win the blessing of their ancestor. Had he lived, he could not have performed any public service. The voice whose tones had so often echoed in the forum was gone, and his feeble limbs could no longer bear his weight. His duty was done. His orations for the crown had all been delivered ; and that crown had been won and worn for half a century with the modesty which became a wise and virtuous statesman of a republic ; and when it was about to be taken from his brow to be garnered for the coming ages, its flowers were fresh, and, like those which the muse of Milton strewed about the walks of Eden, were without a thorn. He had run a long and glorious course. His duty was all done. He had taken his place in the history of his country.

In the contemplation of such a character, when the keen pang of parting is past, joy should take the place of mourning. Let us rejoice at the prospect which greeted his closing eyes. In his last days he was cheered by the greatness of his country. When he first saw the light, his beloved Virginia was indeed bounded by the Ohio, and had a nominal line on the Missisisppi, the extreme verge of the British claim ; but she was the humble vassal of imperial power. He saw that Virginia, when, retiring from the Danube of the West, she gave independence and position to that lovely region, which, under the name of Kentucky, became her equal in the federal union. He saw that Virginia, beneath the banner of the gallant Clark, dipping her feet in the waters of the Northern lakes ; and he saw her cede to the confederation that vast North-western domain with the single provision that states as free and as sovereign as herself should be carved from its territory ; and he saw those states, one by one, take their station in the American Union. When he was born, the flag of Britain streamed from the old Capitol in his native city, and flapped above his head ; and in the South the St. Mary's was the extreme limit of British territory. He lived to see that flag the trophy of his country, and to see the stars and stripes wave above the waters of the Mexican gulf, and over those of the Atlantic and Pacific seas. He lived to see our numbers swell from three millions to more than thirty-one millions ; and our commerce which at his birth was confined to a few ports of Britain float on every sea, and freighted with the wealth of every clime. He saw our extended country flourishing, beyond the example of so young a nation in ancient or in modern times, in the arts and sciences, in knowledge and in power and in true religion. And, with such a scene before him, he closed his eyes in peace.

Let us remember ourselves, and inculcate upon our children the lessons of so august a life. Let us point them to his pure and studious youth, and his love of those who taught him, weeping at the age of eight in parting from his young tutor, whom he was to meet again; and later as his rival and equal at the bar; and later still when both, having attained the highest honors of the profession, had retired from its walks; and later still, when half a century had elapsed, he closed a tender and life-long friendship at his grave. Let us point to him, unguarded by a parent's care from his third year, that parent one of the master-spirits of a great Revolution and ever absent in his fearful work, remarkable for his correct deportment and that perseverance in well-doing so strikingly shown by the fact that he, alone among his young contemporaries, finished his studies at college with the approbation of the faculty, and received the only degree conferred upon his class. Let us point our youth to the zeal with which he sought instruction in useful knowledge; how, a mere boy, almost imperceptibly, it may be in the office of his grandfather, or of Mr. Wythe, or of Mr. Wickham, or of the General Court, but some how, somewhere, perhaps drawn on the instant from the philosophy of the law, he acquired a thorough knowledge of all the mysteries and learning of a clerk of a court—a mastery so thorough, that in after years he was consulted by the most eminent clerks in difficult cases in their calling; and how he not only mastered that department of knowledge, but studied its mere mechanical details, and learned that beautiful hand which was conspicuous in all his writings. Let us recall to them the industry with which he, the heir-apparent of a fortune, which, however, he never received, pursued the study of the law; how, by his moral purity, his intelligence, and his becoming deportment, he won, a mere youth, the confidence and the intimacy of some of the most distinguished men of that age; and how he heeded the lessons which he heard from their lips, and imitated the singular virtues which shone in their lives. Let us recall the fact, so patent in his life, and so cheering to the young and virtuous of every land, that moral worth and abilities will ever be promptly recognized by those true patrons of the age—the People—who took the young Tazewell in charge, who, at the age of one-and-twenty, sent him to the Assembly, and who, as soon as he was eligible to a seat in the House of Representatives, conferred upon him that most distinguished honor in their gift and placed him in the chair of John Marshall. Let us call the attention of our young men to the next great step in his life, when, having obtained the highest political honors which could be conferred on so young a man, realizing that a competent fortune was the solid basis of independence moral and political, and that the family hearth was the true home of human happiness, he let the cup of ambition pass from him, and devoted himself to the practical business of life. And then let us unfold before our youth his splendid career at the bar—a career radiant with genius, marked by untiring industry and fidelity to the interests confided to his care, brilliant with extraordinary displays of intellect, upheld by dauntless courage, memorable as well by his triumphant successes as by the moderation of his fees and by the moral light which he diffused around him, regarding, as he ever did, rapacity, extortion, and complicity in evil-doing as the worst of crimes, and more memorable, as blending in a single character, and at an early age, those uncommon qualities which separately make the reputation of a great advocate, of a great civilian, and of a great master of the Laws of Nations; and, more memorable still, when, his high position attained, and able to add thousands upon thousands to his wealth, he, with noble self-denial, put another enticing cup away from his lips, and withdrew with a moderate competence only to the bosom of his family and to the peaceful pursuits of agriculture, leaving, as an example worthy of all imitation, a broad margin which Plutus might have condemned, but which Socrates, Cato, and Cicero would have extolled, between the bar of man and that supreme tribunal before which we must all appear; how, when in the retirement which he so much loved, his country called for his services, he promptly and generously rendered them, serving a long term of years, speaking, accustomed as he was to speak, rarely, but effectively and conclusively, so that nothing was to be said after him, and winning laurels for himself in the high places of the land, and from the foremost spirits of the age—laurels whose only worth in his eyes was that he might lay them at the feet of that blessed mother of us all, our beloved Virginia; how, when he had performed long and distinguished service abroad, which Virginia and the whole country were anxious to reward, he again sought retirement, relinquishing without a sigh to others those personal honors which so fascinate the votaries of ambition, but which had no charm for him; how, when he had formed with the utmost deliberation his political creed, he adhered most closely and conscientiously, and in the face of great temptations, to its cardinal doctrines throughout his entire course; yet, throning country above party in the empire of his affections, he did not hesitate to oppose as readily and as fearlessly his political friends when he deemed them wrong as he sustained them when he believed them to be right; how, though a stern upholder of the public honor, he ever sought to avoid war, when it was consistent with the public interests to defer it, and, in 1807, when a false step on his part would have brought on an instant rupture with Great Britain, he, with consummate tact and courage, poured oil upon the troubled waters, and averted a war which, under the circumstances, would have been worse than a civil war—*bellum plus quam civile*—a war to the knife; how, at a later day, when, on the eve of the conclusion of the war in Europe, it was resolved to commence hostilities with England, he sought to postpone the struggle for a season, convinced that a short delay would render it unnecessary, and how signally his foresight was justified by the result; thus recommending, in opposition to the pervading sentiment of the State, a policy which would have saved thousands of valuable lives, and a hundred millions of money, expended in our contest with England; how, at a still later day, when the Senate of the United States, unconsciously and needlessly, were about to involve us in a war with Spain, his eloquence rescued the country from the impending danger; yet, when war was declared against his will, ever ready to unite with his countrymen in prosecuting hostilities with the greatest vigor; how, alone among all the departed statesmen of Virginia, he managed, with the industry and attention of an ordinary citizen, his private affairs, into which he introduced a system which the planter and the merchant might wisely imitate, and which enabled him to compete with his most skilful contemporaries in the success which followed all his exertions; how, unseduced by a love of gold in an age of speculation, he never committed a dollar to the caprices of fortune, or lost an investment;

how, though affluent with wealth, won mainly by downright industry and waxing greater every hour by the force of that wondrous element in the accumulation of money, a lengthened lapse of years, he constantly and steadily turned his back upon the extravagance and social follies of the day, and exhibited in his household and in his life those stern and sterling virtues of prudence, economy, and thrift, which were the characteristics of the early fathers of the republic; displaying before the eyes of the people a model wherein the loftiest genius, the most varied and profound learning, the most fervid patriotism ever sinking self in country, the severe simplicity and frugality which should ever shine along the track of a true republican statesman, and an escutcheon undebased by a solitary vice, were united in all their fair and grand proportions; how, in his happy home, he dispensed, freely and without price, the marvellous stores of learning and experience which he had amassed during his long and eventful career, turning his modest study into a chamber of philosophy, and the well-spring of oracles more practical, more prudent, more profound, and penetrating further into the abyss of the dark and illimitable future than were ever uttered at the Pythian fane; and last, though not least, how, in the lingering twilight of his years as in their earliest dawn, he loved Virginia, not with that cold feeling which looks to latitude and longitude, to East or to West, as the limits of affection, but, first, in that tender and household light, as the home of his ancestry, the sepulchre of his sires, his own birth and burial-place, and the birth and burial-place of those who were dear to him, and then in that more majestic aspect as the bride of liberty, the first-born of the colonies of Britain, and the first born of the States of the new world, as the mother of heroes, statesmen, and philosophers, "above all Greek, above all Roman fame," as the sole mistress of his heart, valuing her humblest commission, whether stamped by the greater or the lesser seal, above the highest honors which a federal executive could bestow, or the most gorgeous transcript of imperial praise, as a free, puissant, and perfect commonwealth, as an integral, independent, and sovereign State, as independent, as sovereign, as when she struck the lion with his senseless motto from her flag, and placed in their stead her own Virtue, erect, with a helmet on her head, a spear in her hand, and a fallen crown at her feet, and that ever dear and ever living sentiment, "SIC SEMPER TYRANNIS," and especially and touchingly, with unutterable and inextinguishable affection, as the beneficent parent who had rocked his cradle, who had held out to him in youth the helping hand, who had honored his meridian and his setting years with her greenest bays, and who, as he humbly and fondly hoped, would drop a tear upon his tomb, and hold his name not unworthy of her remembrance. Let us, gentlemen, recall these and similar traits of this illustrious man, and holding up before posterity his pure and bright example, let us not only honor it with our tongues, but imprint it on our hearts, and imitate it in our lives.

And now, Patron of my youth, Guide and Counsellor of my maturer years, and ever, ever, ever the Friend of my bosom, HAIL and FAREWELL!

APPENDIX.

No. I.

Proceedings of the Bar of Norfolk on the death of Mr. Tazewell.

No. II.

Correspondence Concerning the Publication of Mr. Grigsby's Discourse.

No. III.

Characters of Mr. Tazewell, by the Hon. George Loyall; by the late William Wirt, Attorney General of the United States; by the late Francis Walker Gilmer, Esq., Professor of Law in the University of Virginia; and by William W. Sharp, Esq.

No. IV.

Extracts from the Letters of Mr. Tazewell concerning Public Office.

No. V.

The Funeral of Mr. Tazewell.

No. VI.

Portraits of Mr. Tazewell.

APPENDIX.

No. I.

PROCEEDINGS OF THE BAR OF NORFOLK, VIRGINIA, ON THE DEATH OF MR. TAZEWELL.

MEETING OF THE NORFOLK BAR.

At a meeting of the members of the Norfolk Bar, held in the Court-room, May 7, 1860, on the motion of Tazewell Taylor, James R. Hubard was called to the Chair, and Chas. Sharp and John T. Francis appointed Secretaries.

William W. Sharp offered the following preamble and resolutions, which were unanimously adopted:

The members of the Bar of Norfolk, having learned that Littleton Waller Tazewell, Esq., died at his residence, in this city, yesterday morning, in the 86th year of his age, have assembled to express their feelings on the occasion of the demise of such an illustrious member of their body. More than the third of a century has elapsed since, crowned with its highest honors, he retired from the profession; and the reflection is as apposite as it is solemn, that not a member of the present bar was his contemporary; but, though he was nominally withdrawn from active life, his presence in our city, his great accessibility to all who chose to consult him, the exuberance of his vast stores of knowledge, which came forth freely at the call of his friends, his splendid parliamentary career, his overshadowing reputation which, as it was felt and universally acknowledged by his associates at the Bar of Virginia, loomed yet larger through the haze of years—these and his fine social qualities ever kept him fresh in the eyes and in the hearts of his professional successors. Thus it was, that though so long withdrawn from the field of his meridian fame, he seemed to be connected with us by a sensible and living tie; and thus it is that we feel more acutely the loss which our body, which our city, and which our common country, have experienced in his death.

It was a severe but touching sentiment of an ancient poet, that no man ought to be deemed happy before his death; and such is the instability of human affairs, so sudden and unexpected are human events and opinions, there is too much room for belief in the mournful reflection; but, if the case of any individual may be singled out as an exception, it was that of Mr. Tazewell. He had reached the highest fame that has been attained at the Bar of Virginia and of the Union; and with the laurels gathered in forensic contests, he had interwoven those which he won on the floor of the Senate of the United States. His wise economy, his financial skill, and his sound practical judgment, had amassed a fortune which increased with every year: and, as if nothing should be wanting to his felicity, he was blessed with a large and lovely family, the bride of his youth, until within a year past, still diffusing around her the light of her early love, and children and grandchildren awaiting his blessing. The very seclusion in which he lived was an element of peace and serenity in his latter days. He interfered with no man's schemes; he thwarted the ambition of no aspirant; in the vigor of manhood, and in the prime of his extraordinary powers, he had put the cup of rivalry and ambition by; and no persuasion or inducement would have led him to press its lips as his sands were running low. Hence, unbiassed by the prejudices of the hour, unswayed by the flattering schemes of personal interests, he brought his great powers to bear upon current questions with a force that it was hard to resist or elude, and with a sagacity almost prophetic. But that force will be felt now no more: that sagacity will cease to sway the judgments of men; and Death has placed its seal upon his destiny; and it has become our sad office to lament his loss:—Therefore, be it

Resolved, That, while we feel painfully the death of so illustrious a member of our profession, we are grateful to the Disposer of Events that, with all his noble faculties unimpaired, and in the midst of untold temporal blessings, our deceased brother attained to such an advanced age, and reflected for so many years upon the Bar, upon his native and beloved Commonwealth, and upon the Union at large, the lustre of his splendid talents, the pure and unsullied glory of his name and fame, and his eminent moral and social virtues.

Resolved, That the members of the Bar will this day attend his funeral in a body; and wear crape on the left arm for thirty days.

Resolved, That Hugh Blair Grigsby be requested to prepare a discourse on the life and character of Mr. Tazewell, to be delivered before the Bar at such time as may suit his convenience.

Resolved, That we extend to the family of our deceased brother our warmest and most heartfelt condolence on the death of its illustrious head.

Resolved, That a copy of these proceedings be presented to the family of Mr. Tazewell.

Resolved, That these resolutions be published in the newspapers of Norfolk and Richmond.

After the reading of the above resolutions, Messrs. Tazewell Taylor, Hugh Blair Grigsby, William W. Sharp, and L. H. Chandler, delivered touching and appropriate addresses.

On motion of William W. Sharp, the blank in the third resolution was filled with the name of Hugh Blair Grigsby, who, being present, accepted the appointment.

The meeting then adjourned to enable the members of the Bar to attend the funeral.

JAMES R. HUBARD, *Chairman.*

CHARLES SHARP, }
JOHN T. FRANCIS, } *Secretaries.*

No. II.

CORRESPONDENCE CONCERNING THE PUBLICATION OF MR. GRIGSBY'S DISCOURSE.

NORFOLK, JUNE 29, 1860.

HUGH B. GRIGSBY, ESQ.:

SIR:—On behalf of the Norfolk bar, the undersigned committee desire to express to you their thanks for the able and interesting discourse on the life and character of the late Littleton Waller Tazewell, Esq., delivered before the bar this morning, and request a copy thereof for publication.

Expressing the hope that you will find it convenient and agreeable to comply with the request,

We are, sir, with great respect, your ob't serv'ts,

W. W. SHARP,
JNO. S. MILLSON,
TAZEWELL TAYLOR,
HN. ROBERTSON,
JNO. T. FRANCIS,
} Committee.

NORFOLK, JUNE 29, 1860.

GENTLEMEN:—In complying with your request for a copy of my discourse, delivered this morning, it is proper that I should state the circumstances under which it was prepared. When I accepted from the bar the office of delivering a discourse on the life and character of Mr. Tazewell, I said to the meeting that, from the state of my eyes, I could not probably prepare it before the fall; but, having been unexpectedly detained in Norfolk beyond my usual time of leaving it for the country, and fearing from the state of my own health and from the uncertainty of human affairs, that, if I postponed the discourse till the fall, I might be prevented from preparing it then, I determined to do the work, as well as I could, at once, and the result is the discourse of which I read a portion to you this morning.

It is hastily written, and written almost wholly from my own mind, and, I may add, for the meridian of Virginia; but I have ventured to send it to you, such as it is, and I indulge the hope that, humble as it is, it may serve to recall, in some slight measure at least, and until some better memorial be prepared, the recollections of a statesman who was long the pride of his native commonwealth, and who stood to most of you in the intimate and endearing relation of a personal friend.

I am, gentlemen, with the highest respect, very truly yours,

HUGH BLAIR GRIGSBY.

To W. W. SHARP,
JOHN S. MILLSON,
TAZEWELL TAYLOR,
HARRISON ROBERTSON,
JOHN T. FRANCIS,
} Esquires, Committee of the Norfolk Bar.

No. III.

CHARACTERS OF MR. TAZEWELL, BY THE HON. GEORGE LOYALL; BY WILLIAM W. SHARP, ESQ., A PUPIL OF MR. TAZEWELL; BY THE LATE WILLIAM WIRT, ATTORNEY GENERAL OF THE UNITED STATES; AND BY THE LATE FRANCIS WALKER GILMER, ESQ., PROFESSOR OF LAW IN THE UNIVERSITY OF VIRGINIA.

The sketch of Mr. Tazewell by Mr. Loyall appeared under the editorial head of the *Norfolk Argus*, on the 8th of May. It was written in haste, but it shows the impression which Mr. Tazewell made on that able and accomplished gentleman. None had a longer or a fairer view of Mr. Tazewell for forty-five years past than Mr. Loyall, and it was mainly owing to him that Mr. Tazewell was brought forward as a candidate for a seat in the Senate of the United States.

[From the *Norfolk Argus* of May 8, 1860. By the Hon. George Loyall.]

DEATH OF EX-GOV. TAZEWELL.

On Sunday, 11 o'clock A. M., LITTLETON WALLER TAZEWELL breathed his last. It was in the Providence of God to prolong the life of this venerable and distinguished man beyond the term of four-score years, during which the beams of his genius irradiated the land of his birth. Among the last, if not the very last, of a noble and vigorous stock, to whom Virginia owes so much of her well-deserved fame, the main features of his character, as was said of an illustrious statesman of the last century, had the hardihood of antiquity.

It was impossible to behold Mr. Tazewell—his majestic form and massive brow—without a vivid impression of the superiority of his intellectual powers; and this impression was invariably deepened whenever a suitable occasion called for their exercise. It may be truly said that he was coeval with the outburst of our Revolutionary struggle, the period of his birth having preceded but a year or two the Declaration of Independence. After a thorough preparatory discipline, we find his name inscribed on the catalogue of William and Mary College, contemporary with those of John Thompson (Curtius) of Petersburg, John Randolph of Roanoke, Robert B. Taylor of this place, and other kindred spirits. He entered upon his professional career at a period when the bar of our State was thronged with men of extensive learning and the highest order of abilities. His success was not long a matter of doubt or speculation. Unambitious of distinction, in the commonly received sense, and unwilling to leave, even for a time, the comparatively humble field of his habitual labors, yet when summoned away to some new or larger theatre, (in the meridian of his fame it not unfrequently happened,) his efforts were marked by extraordinary brilliancy and power. It was universally conceded that, when roused upon such occasions to put forth his whole strength, the more strenuous and stern the combat, the more signal his triumph.

As was remarked of Lord Mansfield, so with Mr. Tazewell, the shackles of a law education and profession, perhaps, formalized, and, in some degree, repressed the splendor of his genius; still, whether in the senate chamber, the hall of legislation, or the court-room, his "speaking was the full expression of the mighty thought, the strong triumphant argument, the rush of native eloquence." His calm dignity and colossal strength, his luminous masculine and searching logic, the vast extent and variety of his research, the large stores of his affluent knowledge, marshalled and arranged with consummate skill and judgment, together with the fascination of his purely unaffected, earnest manner, the magic power of his unstudied action, and the thrilling intonations of his deep rich voice, rendered him, in his best days, "before public assemblies, almost irresistible." He managed his strength to such advantage, that few men dared to grapple with him "in a pitched field of long and serious debate." His general tone and style in debate were marked by an intense earnestness, whilst his narrative, possessing, from its striking naturalness and simplicity, a high degree of dramatic interest, was occasionally relieved with splendid passages of impassioned and stirring eloquence. Intrepid self-reliance, unwearied activity, far-reaching sagacity, clearness, and fulness, were the prominent characteristics of Mr. Tazewell's mind. Comprehending with intuitive glance the whole field of argument, he "launched into his subject like an eagle dallying with the wind." One of our leading statesmen declared, upon a memorable occasion, that "Tazewell was second to no man that breathed." Certainly, it is no exaggeration to say that, for robust discipline, vigorous reasoning, grasp and amplitude of thought, he was almost without a rival.

Virginia had conferred upon him her highest official trusts. Her generous confidence he requited with a deep and fervent devotion, laying upon the altar of her stern and simple political faith the offerings of matured wisdom, and upholding, in all seasons, with a lofty patriotism and the utmost energies of his powerful intellect, her right and honor. Standing upon the great principles that lie at the foundation of our institutions, the powers of the Federal Government, as limited and defined by the Compact, and the rights of the States in all their integrity, he regarded as vital to the preservation of the Confederacy and the stability of our republican system. Whether in repelling open assaults upon the Constitution, or meeting at the threshold covert abuses of delegated power, no man within our border saw more clearly, or more directly and firmly trod the path of duty before him. Personal asperities engendered by political strife, and which too often follow in the train of collisions of opinion and partisan warfare, were "alien to his nature." In his retirement from the public arena, during the last twenty years or more, he sympathized but little with the busy world.

Of most happy temperament, and without a particle of ostentation or parade, "his spirit was finely touched with the gentler virtues," and those who enjoyed the privilege of his social intimacy will remember with delight the unaffected frankness and simplicity of his manners, the varied range, the breadth and depth and vivacity of his "marvellously rich and beautiful conversation," whilst they must deeply deplore the loss of one as remarkable for mildness and the kindliest affections in his domestic relations, and all the intercourse of private life, as for profound thought and rare attainments.

It is not the purpose, nor is it within the scope of this brief memorial, to delineate the character of this eminent citizen. *Clarum et venerabile nomen*—"a fairer tribute shall one day grace his honorable tomb." He belongs now to history.

SKETCH OF MR. TAZEWELL BY MR. SHARP.

This sketch appeared in one of the morning papers of Norfolk on the 8th of May; and though hastily written, deserves to be republished here. Mr. Sharp is the only member of the bar now living who was a student in the office of Mr. Tazewell, and who saw him closely while engaged in the two or three last years of his practice at the bar.

The mortal career of our celebrated townsman, Littleton Waller Tazewell, closed on Sunday morning, at 11 o'clock. He was emphatically one of the great men of his age, and a just memorial of his life will, no doubt, be specially prepared in due season. Meantime, we will note, that he was born in the city of Williamsburg, where his father, Judge Tazewell, of the Court of Appeals, subsequently resided, on the 17th of December, 1774. After finishing his education at William and Mary College, he commenced his study of the law, partly under the care of his grandfather, Mr. Waller, and the late Mr. Wickham, of Richmond. He was distinguished at once at the bar as scientifically acquainted with his profession, the principles of which he drew, not from the labor-saving indexes of the present day, but from the pure and almost sacred writings of Coke and Mansfield. Such wells of truth were not sounded except by great intellectual efforts, and it is chiefly owing to the necessity which then existed of making such efforts, that we boast of the great lawyers of past times.

In a short time after his appearance in the courts he was elected to the Legislature, and was one of its members in the great session of '98, when the resolutions prepared by Mr. Madison were introduced. The next year he represented the Williamsburg District in Congress, being successor to Judge Marshall in that body, and was present during the stormy period of Mr. Jefferson's election to the Presidency over Burr. Few statesmen have more truly appreciated the grandeur of Mr. Jefferson's teachings than did the subject of this notice.

He declined a reëlection to Congress, and came to Norfolk in 1802, then a place of extensive foreign commerce, and soon entered upon a large and important practice. During the same year he married a daughter of the late Col. Nivison, and from that time to the present continued to reside among us. With the exception of the interrupting years of the war of 1813–14, and of a short period, during which he represented this city in the Legislature on a special occasion, he practised his profession with the honor and success that were to have been expected from one who was, while yet a young man, pronounced by Judge Marshall and Judge Roane to be unsurpassed, if equalled, by any competitor of his day. It was indeed hard to speak in measured terms of a lawyer who, though a resident of a provincial town, was consulted, at the same time, (1819,) by London merchants on the "custom of London," and by the priests of Rome on the canon law.

At the earnest solicitation of Mr. Monroe, he reluctantly accepted the appointment of one of the commissioners under the Florida treaty,—being united in that duty with Mr. King and the late Hugh Lawson White; and after that work was done, he withdrew from the practice of law to the privacy which he so much, perhaps too much, loved.

In 1825 he was elected by the General Assembly a Senator of the United States over some distinguished competitors, and soon after taking his seat was called upon to discuss the celebrated Piracy bill of Mr. Monroe's administration; and in a speech on that measure, which he defeated, displayed such extraordinary resources of argument and learning as threw all his associates of that epoch in the shade, and established his own reputation as the greatest debater of his age.

He was a prominent member of the Convention of Virginia in 1829–30, where his compeers were Chief Justice Marshall, John Randolph, Watkins Leigh, Taylor, Upshur, and others of that brilliant assembly. He was at the same time a Senator from Virginia in Congress; and was in nothing behind the great personages of the Senate, where sat Calhoun, Clay, and Webster, save only in his invincible desire and love of retirement.

In 1833–4 he resigned his seat in the Senate of the United States, and soon after, and almost without his knowledge, he was elected Governor of Virginia, the duties of which office he actively and faithfully performed until his resignation, which took place before the expiration of his term.

From that time he has continued in private life—but not uselessly, for he has been consulted from all parts of the Union on almost all subjects; and by his intimate acquaintances, his opinions have been regarded as oracular inspirations. He has also attended with care to his private duties, and these, with his correspondence, have chiefly occupied his later years.

It has been the subject of deep regret that one possessing such colossal powers should have been so unwilling to exert them. There is but one instance in history of a really great man seeking an obscurity which he could not win, —the case of Chief Justice Wilmot, of England. But Mr. Tazewell had the right to judge and decide for himself, and that he preferred private to public life is rather to be lamented than complained of. Nor must it be supposed that this preference was the effect of indolence. On the contrary, he was, in his way, a laborious man, and it may be that the leisure of his latter years may have been productive of important fruits in literature and science to those who have survived him.

We will not, and need not, dwell upon the private relations of Mr. Tazewell, in all of which he had no superior; and although for many years he has been a stranger upon our streets, yet we feel that even in a social point of view we have sustained a loss which cannot be repaired. There is great sadness in our city, which pervades all its ranks, and which even those who never saw him deeply feel. We add no more than to offer our unaffected sympathy to his family.

DESCRIPTION OF MR. TAZEWELL, BY THE LATE WILLIAM WIRT, ATTORNEY GENERAL OF THE UNITED STATES.

This sketch of Mr. Tazewell is taken from the twenty-fourth number of the OLD BACHELOR, a name given to a series of papers written in imitation of The Spectator, The Rambler, and their successors, and designed to improve the morals and elevate the taste of the community. They appeared in the Richmond Enquirer during the years 1813–14, and were republished in duodecimo in the latter year. Mr. Tazewell is represented as a youth of twenty-two, under the name of Sidney; Gen. Taylor under that of Herbert; the late Judge Parker under that of Alfred; the late Francis W. Gilmer under that of Galen I believe; and I suspect Mr. Wirt himself is the Old Bachelor of the piece. But, for various reasons, I shall only present Mr. Tazewell as he appears in the character of Sidney. As Mr. Wirt was Clerk of the House of Delegates for three years of the time during which Mr. Tazewell was a member of the body, he must have known personally Mr. Tazewell in his twenty-second or third year; and although the sketch was written fourteen or fifteen years later, it may have been drawn from actual life.

"On the night of the arrival of the young friends mentioned in my former number, Alfred, whose signal had drawn them to the parlor, where they were first met by Rosalie and myself, performed the part of master of ceremonies by giving us a mutual introduction, which he did in the following terms:

"'My friends, this is Dr. Cecil, the benevolent censor of the age; and this is my sister Rosalie. This, sir,' addressing me, 'is the son of a man whom I have often heard you admire, Mr. Sidney;' presenting a spare young man of good figure, whose face seemed formed on the finest model of antiquity, and whose large eye, of a soft deep blue, habitually expanded, as if looking upon a wide and boundless surface, might well be called *an eye of ocean.* He advanced with mild and graceful composure, and saluted me with an unassuming modesty and politeness, blended at the same time with a manly firmness, simplicity, and dignity, which gave me the presentiment that he was a superior character."

After describing a conversation in which Van Tromp, Reynolds, Herbert, and Sidney took part, the narrative continues:

"But Sidney's appeared to be the master-spirit; cool, collected, firm, vigorous, and self-balanced, he stood, like an eagle upon the rocks of Norway's coast, defying with equal composure the storm that raved and rent the atmosphere above, and the surging element that towered and dashed and roared below.

"This young man was really a prodigy. He was only two-and-twenty years of age; yet his information seemed already to be universal. He spoke on every science and every art like one of its ablest professors. There was no broken lumber nor useless trash in his mind. The materials were all of the best sort, and in the highest order. The stores of his knowledge had been collected with so much reflection and hypothetical application, and arranged in his memory with so much skill and method, that he would call them into use at a moment's warning; and there was no point which he wished to illustrate by analogy, or support by a precedent, for which his memory did not supply him at once with the happiest materials.

"There were one or two important particulars in which he had a manifest and striking advantage over the generality of young men. Where, for instance, Herbert, Reynolds, and Van Tromp had, through indolence or hurry, passed over the Gordian knots which had occurred in the course of their studies, Sidney seems to have stopped, and sitten deliberately and patiently down, resolved not to cut but to untie them before he rose, so as not only to make himself master of the knowledge which they concealed, but to discover also how the knot came to be tied; whether it arose from the unavoidable difficulty of the subject, or from the want of care or of intellectual strength in the author. Thus he trained and practised his mind to grapple with difficulties and to subdue them; and thus he gave to his penetration a point of adamant which no difficulty could stop or turn aside.

"But, besides this temper of superior hardihood and vigor with which he thus endued his mind, there was this further advantage from this process: that his knowledge was much superior both in quantity and accuracy. Sidney's course of study had resembled a cloudless day in which all was light and every object visible, whether on hill, plain, or in dale; whereas theirs resembled a coruscation by night, in which only the most prominent objects are seen, and that, too, only by sudden and transient glimpses. And hence, I remarked, that very often in the course of their conversation, when they were under the eclipse of one of those Gordian knots, lost in valleys, shade, and darkness, Sidney was in broad and perfect day.

"It was owing, too, as I believe, to the ever-wakeful, intense, and ardent action of the mind, as well as the collateral meditation and study with which he had read, that his memory appeared to have possessed a faculty of discriminating among the subjects offered to its retention, and rejecting the incumbrance of what was worthless, to have seized and holden with indissoluble tenacity everything that was useful, *together with all its roots and ramifications.* He seems to have examined the historical incidents with which he had met, with all that 'large, sound, round-about sense,' as Mr. Locke calls it, which was necessary to combine with it all its causes and consequences, and render it practically useful to the purposes of life. I was several times struck with the superior advantages which he derived from these details of relative and antecedent with which he had recorded in his memory historical facts. His fellow-students were acquainted with all the prominent incidents of history; but not having examined them in all their bearings, as they had read, and impressed them, *with all their relations of cause and effect*, on their minds, it turned out that they frequently attempted to borrow aid from historical incidents, which Sidney, from his more intimate knowledge and mastery of the subjects, was able to seize and drive back upon them like routed elephants upon their own army.

"He surpassed them, too, in those powers which are derived from mathematical study; the power of keeping continually in the mind's eye, without winking or wavering, the distant proposition which is to be proven; of advancing to it by steady steps on the shortest route; and bearing up, with the strength of Atlas, the most extended and ponderous chain of logical deductions. Such was the habitual steadiness and strength of his mind, that, unlike his fellow-students, I never saw him lose sight, for an instant, of the point in debate, much less shift that point to something else; in advancing to it, I never saw him take one devious step; nor did I ever see him at any moment oppressed or entangled by the concatenation of his argument, or indicate even that he was at all sensible of its weight.

"That there may have been something in the original organization of his mind or temperament of his character, that qualified him, in a preëminent degree, for cool, dispassionate, profound, and vigorous exertion, I will not take upon me to deny; but that he owed much more of his excellence to that secret and persevering labor to which he had so nobly submitted, and by which he had given additional tone and power to his mind itself, I am perfectly convinced. His mind did, now, indeed, appear in itself the superior one; it had such a power of compression and expansion, of versatility and strength, that it seemed capable of anything and everything that he pleased. It was astonishing with what rapidity and effect he would shift the color, shape, and attitude of the same object as the emergencies of his argument required. With what closeness and unanswerable cogency he would maintain truth! and with what illusion and almost irrefutable sophistry he would disguise and metamorphose error! At the first sound of the trumpet he could draw a larger body of forces into the field in favor of an erroneous position than his adversaries could in favor of a correct one; and even when on the wrong side, which he seemed just as willing to be as he was to be on the right, he was generally astute enough to drive his adversaries into straits and keep the field himself in token of victory. Indeed the spirit of enterprise and the consciousness of his strength led him generally to prefer the wrong side to the right, and to support error with more vivacity and appearance of enjoyment than he did truth. His fault seemed to consist in the abuse of his strength; in that laxity of colloquial morals (if I may use the phrase) of which I have just spoken, and which led him to triumph, with equal pleasure, in every victory, right or wrong.

"There was, however, something still more unfortunate in this bold and commanding character, but which I believe I should never have discovered had I not endeavored to take the place of the public towards him, and judge of him as I have seen them judge of others: I mean an apparent frigidity of manner which I feared the world would consider as the evidence of a cold and sordid heart.

"The man who is in possession of such talents as Sidney's, is in possession of a most dangerous gift; and it behoves him to walk before the public with a circumspection proportionate to the superiority of those talents. Exorbitant power, whether intellectual or political, naturally begets distrust and jealousy in the good as well as envy in the wicked; and it requires on the part of its possessor a constant display, not only of the most scrupulous integrity and sacred purity on every occasion, great or small; but a constant display also of the most disinterested generosity and public spirit, to give such a character even fair play before the world. People must be satisfied that such an one will not abuse his power to their injury, and sacrifice their interests to his own; but that the strong and native tendency of his character is to disregard his own interests entirely when drawn into collision with theirs, before they will forgive him his superiority, and trust themselves in his hands. To such a character, any appearance or suspicion of coldness, or indifference towards the public good, and much more any appearance or suspicion of uncommon devotion to self, however fallacious such appearance or suspicion may be, is political death, without the hope of resurrection. Such a character must lose sight of self altogether, compared with the public, or the public will be very apt to lose sight of him, or seeing, not to trust him. As to Sidney, knowing him as I do, I know that those appearances of which I have spoken are entirely fallacious; that his laxity in conversation is only sportiveness; that his attention to his own interests does not surpass the bounds of ordinary prudence; that, on a proper occasion, no man is more charitable, generous, or munificent; none more alive to the misfortunes and even solicitudes of a virtuous sufferer; that his apparent coldness is the effect only of mental abstraction and of judicious caution and reflection; and, in part, of that strong and exhausting flame with which his friendship burns for those whom he grapples to his heart. But the world at large can never have that knowledge of him that I have; and, therefore, though I know that he looks upon mankind with an eye of benevolence, and upon his country with the spirit of a patriot; and though, in addition to this, he is certainly capable of any and every thing that demands fidelity, zeal, energy, industry the most unrelaxing, and talents the most transcendent; yet much I fear his country will never know him well enough to do him justice, or to profit herself of his powers."

SKETCH OF FRANCIS WALKER GILMER.

As the graphic portraiture of Mr. Wirt represents Mr. Tazewell in youth, so the annexed sketch by Mr. Gilmer represents him as he was about to retire from the bar. Mr. Gilmer himself was one of the most brilliant young men Virginia ever produced. That Mr. Jefferson selected him to choose in England the first professors of the University of Virginia—an office which he performed with eminent skill and judgment—is a proof of the estimate which was placed upon his talents by the first men of the age.

The sketch of Mr. Tazewell is taken from a small volume of Mr. Gilmer's productions, published in Baltimore in 1828, page 35.

"I hardly know what apology to make to Littleton W. Tazewell, of Norfolk, for dragging his name from the obscurity which he seems to court, but is unable to win. He has shrunk from the great national amphitheatre, the olympic games, where it is the glory of Mr. Pinkney to challenge and to conquer, to an obscure sea-port town. But, more confident in his powers than he is himself, I do not fear a comparison with this veteran of the bar of the Supreme Court. His person may be a little above the ordinary height, well-proportioned, and having the appearance of great capacity to endure fatigue. His complexion is swarthy, his muscles relaxed as from intense thought long continued. His features are all finely developed. His eyes are large, full, and of a dark blue color, shaded by thick black brows a little raised, as if looking on a vast expanse of distant prospect. A manner firm, manly, dignified, and free. *Vox permanens verum subrauca;* its tremulous and occasionally interrupted accents give unusual tenderness to its tones. But it is neither the Ciceronian person, nor the Chatham face, nor the voice of Antony, that we are to admire in Mr. Tazewell. It is the great and clear comprehension; the freshness and rapidity with which every thing luxuriates on the generous soil of his mind, which is further removed from even occasional sterility than in any one I have known. This soil has no succession of seasons; the sun which warms it is never for a moment obscured by cloud or eclipse; there reigns a bright, a genial, a perpetual summer. His perceptions are as intuitive and as strong as those of Judge Marshall. He has as much intrepidity of intellect as Mr. Pinkney, and great boldness; but no insolence, no exultation of manner. He wants only ambition to make him rival, nay, perhaps even to surpass the accomplished champion of the federal bar. His fault is subtlety, and a provoking minuteness of detail in his argument. He sometimes shows legal and rhetorical artifice where there in not the least occasion for either. These defects, however, have been acquired in the long habit of addressing subordinate tribunals, where his genius riots in its strength, and are so little connected with the original organization of his mind as to be easily cured.

"There is something absolutely painful in reflecting on the destiny of this extraordinary man. Endowed with the best and most various gifts I ever knew concur in any individual; possessing a vast fund of information, and indefatigable in whatever he undertakes; he has a thousand times exhibited talents equal to any occasion, and is still unknown to the world, and, until lately, was almost unheard of beyond the limits of his native State. One may easily reconcile to his philanthropy that "some mute, inglorious Milton" may rest in every neglected grove, because it requires a strong effort of imagination to suppose the clod of the valley ever to have been "pregnant with celestial fire;" but we have not this comfort to allay our mortification, when we see talents of the purest and brightest ray, united to the noblest qualities of the human heart, emitting their lustre in broad daylight, and to the public eye, unnoticed or forgotten. The sentiment which it excites in one is not so much sympathy with the object as regret for the public loss in not appreciating the rarest gifts of Providence to man. The individual himself seems too elevated to permit a vulgar pity. The world is too contemptible in his eyes to render its praise or its censure matter of interest. Perhaps there is something in this public indifference even congenial to one conscious of the inexhaustible resources and the unconquerable power of his mind. The eagle loves the awful solitude of her sublime cliffs, which remove her far from the importunate chattering and impertinent intrusion of magpies and daws; but it is truly a misfortune to the country that the imperial bird should sleep on her lonely eyrie, and leave the supreme dominion to region kites and mousing owls.

"I had long been curious to see the natural vigor, fertility, and adroitness of Mr. Tazewell contrasted with the consummate art and accomplished prowess of Mr. Pinkney; and participated in the public disappointment, (as I must ever deplore the cause which produced it,) when the death of Mr. Pinkney rendered it impossible, just at the moment that the contest was to take place. But a few days before Mr. Pinkney's death, (a circumstance which probably hastened it,) he had exerted himself very much in the argument of a cause of great interest to his client. Immediately the discussion was over, and while the accents of that *cycnea vox* reverberated in the ears of all who heard the last effort of his eloquence, he began the preparation for his argument with Mr. Tazewell. His application was too intense; his strength, and health, and life, sunk under it; and they who hastened from a distance to witness the competition, beheld anticipated victory and triumph turned into a funeral procession: *O fallacem hominum spem, fragilemque fortunam, et inanes nostras contentiones!*"

The reader will keep in mind that this sketch by Mr. Gilmer was written nearly forty years ago, and before Mr. Tazewell appeared in the Senate of the United States.

No. IV.

EXTRACTS FROM THE LETTERS OF MR. TAZEWELL RESPECTING PUBLIC OFFICE.

Mr. Tazewell kept no copies of his letters to his friends, and I make the subjoined extracts, explanatory of his views respecting public office, wholly from those in my own possession. I may state here that when a commissioner was appointed to Kentucky, in 1823, Mr. Tazewell was consulted on the subject by some of his friends in the General Assembly, and he agreed to undertake the office; but when he heard that the friends of Benjamin Watkins Leigh, his warm personal friend, desired the appointment of that distinguished jurist, he sent a peremptory withdrawal of his name, and urged the nomination of Mr. Leigh. When he believed that the arbiters of the dispute between Kentucky and Virginia would be chosen at large, he suggested the names of Jeremiah Mason of New Hampshire, William Hunter of Rhode Island, and Langdon Cheves of Philadelphia.

In a letter, dated January 1, 1823, he says: "I ask nothing from my country, but there is nothing she should ever require of me in vain. . . As a citizen of Virginia, I hold myself bound at all times to render any aid which it may be within the compass of my poor abilities to offer in furtherance of the rights, the interests, and even the wishes of its government. . . Proud as I should be at being selected as the advocate of my country's rights by the unsolicited voice of her legislature, I could not purchase even this gratification at the expense of any whom I love, esteem, or admire."

Under the date of December, 1822, he writes: "If I know myself, there is no situation within the power of government to bestow which I covet or desire, nor is there one which I would not accept, if the discharge of its duties by me was deemed necessary or useful to my country. I have no ambition to gratify, although I have duties to fulfil."

Under the date of December 9, 1824, he says: "The public interest shall never be postponed to my individual concerns, although ruin to myself may result from it."

When once asked for something like a defence of some parts of his political career, which he declined to give, he said: "There is no act of my whole life, public or private, which I regret; none that I am solicitous should not be scrutinized; none the motives or objects of which I cannot instantly explain, in a way which candor will approve."

On the 1st of December, 1824, he writes: "If I know myself, there is no office, place, or appointment within the gift of man which I wish, and none I would accept save from my native State. To her I have never felt myself at liberty to refuse myself under any circumstances, when she thought proper to call me to her side. But even from her I want nothing but that protection which she affords in common to all her citizens. My gratitude would constrain me to sacrifice everything to obey her wishes." On another occasion, when his creed was called for, he wrote: "As a Virginian, I would willingly suffer this inconvenience and make this sacrifice, and much more, for Virginia; but I should feel myself unworthy of her name, if I did not scorn to stoop to the meanness of blazoning to her view my own merits, which, if they exist at all, none ought to know so well as my countrymen, or to vindicate myself against suspicions which, if without foundation, they ought not to entertain. I cannot, therefore, humiliate myself, or degrade my friends, so far as, at this time of day, and under the circumstances in which I am placed, to furnish you or any other with a confession of my political faith, to be read either in the Richmond church or elsewhere, to the end that I may propitiate its tutelary deity or his ministering priesthood; and as this seems to be the *sine qua non* of my success, I must, therefore, beg leave to decline the nomination."

On the 6th of December, 1826, he writes: "I want no office, place, or appointment under the sun, nor will I ever have any except from the gift of my own State."

It thus appears that, though he was not desirous of holding office, he was always willing and ready to perform at every sacrifice any duty which Virginia might require at his hands.

I wish it had been in my power to present even a brief glance at the labors of Mr. Tazewell, as one of the Commissioners under the Florida treaty of 1819, when, in conjunction with the late Judge Hugh L. White and Mr. King, some important questions were decided; but I had no materials within reach while engaged in preparing the discourse; and my recollections were too vague to be used on such an occasion.

No. V.

THE FUNERAL OF MR. TAZEWELL.

[From the *Norfolk Argus*, of May 8, 1860.]

THE funeral obsequies of Mr. Tazewell, yesterday, were solemn and impressive. An appropriate address was delivered by Rev. Mr. Rodman, of Christ church, and a large concourse of persons followed the remains from the family mansion on Granby street to the wharf, whence they were taken to the Eastern Shore for interment.

Thus a very great man has passed away from our midst—a man who was long and justly honored for his profound learning; surpassed by few, if any, in any country. His mind was an immense and well-stored intellectual repository, whence intelligence, varied, rich, and valuable, was drawn at pleasure or as occasion required. Powerful as an orator, brilliant as a writer, scarcely equalled in his knowledge of the great principles of law, his irresistible grasp of intellect astonished thousands in former days—bright and clear as "the cloudless azure of the upper sky."

The proceedings of the meeting of the members of the bar were very appropriate. All the addresses were eloquent and impressive. The speakers aptly mentioned his splendid and successful career as a lawyer, his wonderful legal acquirements, and irresistible eloquence. One of the gentlemen alluded to the fact that the merchant princes of London and the priests of Rome were among those who sought his opinion upon great and important questions, that had puzzled the astute statesmen of other countries.

The last survivor of a noble intellectual triumvirate, of which Norfolk could boast for a time, surpassing the models of antiquity in power and splendor of forensic triumph, has passed away. That triumvirate is now demolished. Taylor, Wirt, and Tazewell have all passed away; this last and most polished shaft now dimmed—Tazewell—just now gone to the grave, "venerable with the ivy of age, and eloquent of greater than classic memories."

To state more particularly the details of the funeral, for future reference—the religious services were held at the family residence on Granby street, and a large number of our most respectable citizens were present on the occasion. Among them were three of our adopted fellow-citizens, who had been on terms of friendly intercourse with the deceased for nearly sixty years, and who walked from their respective abodes in the city to pay the last act of respect to his memory. The eldest of these venerable men, George McIntosh, Esq., was in his ninety-second year, and the others, William H. Thomson, Esq., and John Southgate, Esq., were over eighty years. When the religious services were ended, a procession was formed, and the hearse was escorted to the steamer Northampton, Captain McCarrick, and the coffin was placed on board. The steamer then left for the county of Northampton, across the bay of Chesapeake, having on board the Rev. Mr. Rodman and the Rev. Dr. Okeson, of the Episcopal church, John N. Tazewell, Esq., the only surviving son of the deceased, three of the daughters of Mr. Tazewell, a number of his grandchildren, the bar of Norfolk and its vicinity, and many of our most venerable fellow-citizens. From accident, the steamer did not reach the landing-place on the opposite shore till nearly dusk, and when the corpse was taken on shore the night had gathered in, and the burial service was read by candle-light. The last scene was one of deep and impressive solemnity.

The vault, which was made only large enough to receive the coffin, was composed of solid slabs of granite united by hydraulic cement, five feet below the surface, and was covered by another slab of granite. The vault was then covered with earth, and was ready to receive the monument, which is soon to be erected. The grave was in an enclosure bounded by iron rails, and containing the tombs of Mrs. Tazewell, the wife of the deceased, of HENRY TAZEWELL, Esq., his eldest son, and of LITTLETON WALLER TAZEWELL, Esq., his youngest son. The burial-ground is on the estate of King's creek, which was given by the deceased to his son, JOHN N. TAZEWELL, Esq., who still owns it, and which holds the remains of a number of the ancestors of Mrs. Tazewell—this last circumstance having led to its selection as a place of sepulchre for the family.

It was the public wish that the body of Mr. Tazewell should be deposited in one of the beautiful cemeteries of Norfolk, a city with which his name had been so long connected, and where the stranger would naturally seek his grave, and, I may add, where the lesson of such a pure and illustrious life might be read in the course of the year by thousands of his countrymen; but the peculiar circumstances of the case rendered the scheme impracticable. I must, however, still indulge the hope that, hereafter, when the insecurity of graves on private estates, so signally represented by our Virginia experience, is fully considered, the descendants of this great man may in due time consent to the removal of his remains and those of the family to some more accessible and less exposed situation.

No. VI.

PORTRAITS OF GOVERNOR TAZEWELL.

1. A miniature of Mr. Tazewell before his marriage in 1802, by an unknown artist. It could not have been good at any period of his life.

2. The portrait by Thomson, taken in 1815, when he was about forty, which is a faithful likeness, and the most intellectual of all his portraits which I have seen.

3. A copy of the above, by Leonard, a pupil of Thomson.

4. A Crayon, by St. Mimin, taken in 1812, from which the engravings of Mr. Tazewell were taken.

5. A portrait by Theodore Kennedy, taken when Mr. Tazewell was about seventy. It has some good touches; but it lacks that high intellectual expression which was always present in the features of the original.

6. A Pastile from the above.

7. A portrait by Bonaud de St. Marcel, taken from a daguerreotype. It represents Mr. Tazewell in his eighty-fourth year, and is under size. It is a faithful copy from the daguerreotype, but it fails entirely to impart that majesty of feature which the face of the original retained to the last.

8. The portrait by Healy, kit-cat size, taken as Mr. Tazewell was in 1830, and designed to be inserted in the painting of the Senate of the United States during the debate on the resolutions of Mr. Foote, of Connecticut. The family of Mr. Tazewell regard this portrait as the finest ever taken of him. I have never seen it; nor has the family ever seen the painting into which it was to be introduced. Mr. Tazewell was fifty-seven or eight at the time.

www.ingramcontent.com/pod-product-compliance
Lightning Source LLC
LaVergne TN
LVHW021421110826
845150LV00007B/2024

* 9 7 8 1 4 2 5 5 0 8 6 8 5 *